An Introduction to MAGIC

141

PROFESSIONAL
TRICKS YOU CAN DO

with coins, cards, silks
and billiard balls. Secrets
of famous stage tricks.

Sherman Ripley

Rare photographs of outstanding magicians.

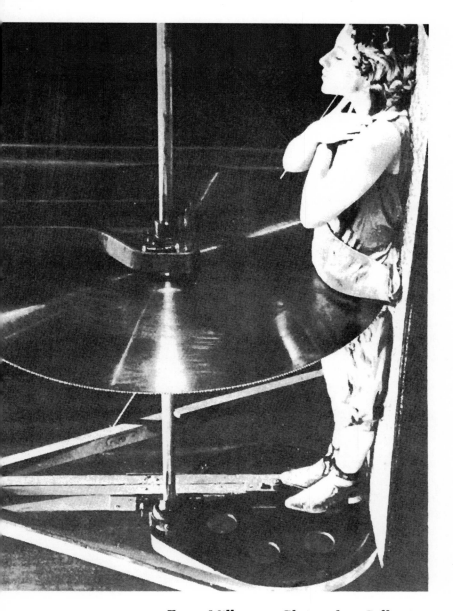

Sawing a woman in half: the most talked-of trick of all times. The subject was originally placed in a box before sawing. Later, the great illusionist, Horace Goldin, perfected a new technique of sawing *without* a covering. The giant buzz-saw "ripped" across her body in full view of the audience; then, she was put back together again—by magic! This is a candid shot of Horace Goldin performing this feat.

CONTENTS

CHAPTER ONE

HOW MAGIC BEGAN

A Glimpse Into Its History

Magic is an ancient art. It precedes written history and is probably contemporaneous with the beginning of folklore. Ancient priests and medicine men practiced crude forms of magic. This is paralleled today in the incantations and taboos of the medicine men of primitive tribes inhabiting remote islands or living in the depths of the jungles. The history of the witch doctor, if uncovered, could well be the history of primitive man.

As civilization advanced, the position of priests, astrologers and soothsayers became increasingly important. They became advisers to kings, generals and tyrants, and rose to high rank and dignity. They were the power behind the throne.

Ancient historians record that the Pharaohs of Egypt maintained court astrologers and magicians who were held in great respect owing to their ability to chart the heavens. They professed also to hold the strange power of foretelling the future. The Bible relates in Exodus that when Aaron cast down his rod before Pharaoh, it became a serpent. This form of magic and other Biblical miracles are beyond our understanding.

The magic of the Orient is traditional. It has held the world enthralled through centuries of folklore and legend. Of such gossamer stuff are spun the tales of the Arabian Nights.

The classic periods of Greece and Rome reflect in their history a profound faith in magic and mystery. The Greeks of the Golden Age and the Romans at the height of their power believed implicitly in their oracles and astrologers. Wizards made prophecies, read the heavens, cast horoscopes and predicted future events. Indeed, they read the will of the gods.

During the reign of King Arthur, legendary British ruler immortalized in story and song by Mallory and Tennyson, a dark and mysterious power in the court was the magician, Merlin. This wizard cast weird spells and uttered magical incantations. Legend states that he had gained these powers from the Druids, an ancient religious sect. By his cunning and occult wisdom he influenced the very life and times of King Arthur's reign.

All through medieval history, a period of superstition and ignorance, a strange array of alchemists sought the "Philosopher's Stone." With this they hoped to transmute baser metals into gold. These magi of the Dark Ages were a mixture of astrologer, faker, chemist and fortune-teller. They sold nostrums, charms, love-potions and for a consideration—poisons. Some, such as the successful charlatan, Cagliostro, prospered on the backwardness and superstitions of that credulous age. Others, however, were sincere and devoted students of science, pioneers in the field of pharmacy, anatomy and chemistry.

As civilization continued to advance, a division of labor and authority arose among the various groups professing higher social functions. The clergy naturally became the interpreters of the wishes and precepts of the Divine Spirit. An enlightened medical profession shouldered the burden of humanity's ills. Fortune-tellers, their prestige greatly deflated, still read futures in cards and teacups. And as for the magician—he continued to perform "miracles!"

The modern magician takes his magic lightly. In our enlightened age he is merely a clever entertainer, a suave and genial actor, playing the part of a man of mystery. He does not profess supernatural powers, but rather admits his trickery. He challenges your intelligence however, and asks you to discover how his illusions are performed.

Perhaps that is why magic will always be popular.

The Value of Magic

To study magic as a hobby is a great satisfaction, and a source of pleasure to oneself and to others. It is truly a rewarding avocation, that may be developed into an art. In studying magic you learn how to stand up before an audience and to express yourself clearly and convincingly, acquiring at the same time poise, self-confidence, grace and assurance. Magic, with all its oddities, makes you a genuine human being. There is an old maxim among magicians: "You don't have to be crazy to be a magician, but it helps!"

The abilities acquired while studying magic are assets for success in life. But, like everything else worth while, they demand exacting study and practice.

The following chapters explain how one can entertain friends with simple and informal magic needing but little study and effort. In time, you will probably want to delve deep into the inner mysteries of this fascinating subject, and develop real skill and dexterity.

First Things First

Do not expect to become a finished artist over night. It is safer too not to saw a lady in half at your first church social. Beginners often try to present tricks before fully mastering them. Better be sure of the trick, the talk, the routine before you present an effect. The secrets of success are study and practice. For magicians, practice before a full-length mirror is most important. Observing yourself from all angles, you see just how to stand, how to hold your arms, and how to make the best impression. The greatest magicians spent long practice periods before mirrors, scrutinizing every move before the presentation of an effect.

Starting Out To Mystify

Never expose magic. Never tell anyone how a trick is done. Any explanation takes away the mystery and spoils the effect of other tricks that you may perform later. "Keep them guessing and send them away laughing."

Misdirection

There's an old saying: "The quickness of the hand deceives the eye." This is only a half-truth. Actually the magician makes his audience look in the wrong place. This is known as misdirection. Here are some practical rules of misdirection:

The audience will look *where you look.*

The audience will look at *anything that moves.*

The audience will look at anything to which you *point.*

The audience will look toward a flash of *light,* a *loud noise,* a *stumble or fall,* a seeming *accident.*

If you hold out your left hand as if there were something in it, and at the same time wiggle the fingers a little, your audience will stare at it. If you look at this hand, and at the same time point at it with your right, the effect will be heightened (Fig. 1). Now, if you toss an imaginary something into the air, at the same time following its flight with your eyes, your audience will do the same. Try this; it is a lesson in misdirection. However you must devise a plausible reason for actions or words that direct the eyes of the audience.

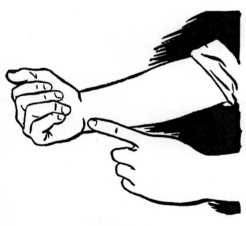

FIGURE 1

The Magician's Clothes

A magician often says, "My pockets are perfectly empty—as usual!" In an ordinary suit the trousers have two large pockets in front and two in back. In the coat there are two large side pockets, a left-hand outer breast pocket and a right-hand inside breast pocket. The vest has two upper and two lower pockets. All of these pockets can be used in magic without any special preparation.

In general, little preparation will be needed in the matter of clothing. However, in a few tricks where this is required, as in the silk production and the billiard ball production, certain special preparations will be described in connection with the trick. Some magicians prefer to entertain with their sleeves rolled up. They slide the coat sleeves up, and the shirt sleeves are turned over them in two or three folds.

Tables and Accessories

Any ordinary small table will do for many tricks. It is best to use a brightly colored cover to throw over your table in order to dress it up a little. Black velvet is useful for concealing things on the table, because black objects are lost against this background. However, some magicians think a black velvet drape or cover looks "tricky." It is therefore better perhaps, to use an "innocent-looking," colored drape and an ordinary-looking table. If you have a small portable table you can rig it up as follows: make a trap by cutting a hole in the front center of it. Hang a pocket below this hole to catch whatever you decide to vanish into the trap. The pocket should be the same color as the drape. This open hole will be invisible a few feet away. It doesn't need to be covered, but the drape must be long enough to cover the pocket from all angles.

You can easily make a servante, or hidden tray for the back of your table. Simply bend a heavy wire in a half-circle, and fasten it at both ends under the back of the table with eyelets or bent nails, so that it slides in and out. When pushed under the table it cannot be seen even from the side. When pulled out it makes a convenient place upon which to vanish any small object. Sew a cloth pocket about an inch and a half deep around the wire frame. This servante slides entirely out of the table when you don't want to use it. Of course there is a section cut out of the back drape to allow for the projection of the servante. Similar servantes may be used on chairs, attached with hooks, wires, thumb tacks or rubber suckers. A box servante is good; it is simply a colorful box from which you take any item needed in your show. You may vanish articles into or behind it by placing a wand or fan across the top of the box.

You can make a good portable table from a music stand. Construct a wooden table-top just big enough to go into your suitcase, or larger if you wish more table area. Take your music stand to a plumber. Have him saw off the holder at the top and substitute a "union" that will screw onto the center of the table top. Add a flashy table drape, and your portable table is complete.

For my own show I carry two rather colorful drapes designed to go on ordinary bridge tables. I borrow the tables in advance. These give me twice as much table space as a "magician's" table.

There are a lot of small gadgets, "fekes," and accessories that magicians use. I shall tell you about these in connection with the tricks in which they are used, and also in a special chapter devoted to the subject.

Patter and Music

The talk or "patter" that accompanies each trick is very important. It should be timed to direct the attention of your audience away from the things they are not supposed to see. "Patter" should be amusing as well as interesting. Put your imagination to work. Tell an amusing story, one that will go

13

with each trick on the program. Also work in a few good jokes or side remarks. Do not take yourself too seriously.

Weave a fanciful tale about your magic and make your stories humorous and light in vein. Successful entertainers, such as Jarrow and Van Hooten, the Mad Magician, presented two or three tricks in the course of their program, but they were so clever in their line of patter that they kept huge audiences in spasms of laughter, and got more applause than some men who were perhaps more skillful. Never forget: "It isn't what you do, but how well you do it." And, "It isn't what *you* like — it's what the *audience* likes."

Certain bits of pure sleight-of-hand and manipulation go well without patter, but rather need a background of light classical music. These presentations are artistic, and lend variety to your program.

Good musical numbers for sleight-of-hand manipulations are "Chinatown" (chorus), "Over the Waves," "Skaters' Waltz," "Anchors Aweigh." The following classics are also excellent: Mendelssohn's "Spring Song," Dvorak's "Humoresque," "Melody in F" by Rubenstein and "Tonight We Love" from Tschaikowsky's "Concerto in B flat Minor." The last is wonderful for a silk production, whereas "Spring Song" is something special for the billiard ball production. Both of these tricks will be described later.

CHAPTER TWO

SILK OF THE ORIENT

Magic with Silk

There is something mysterious about silk. Perhaps it is its oriental origin. Magicians can do wonderful things with it.

Dealers in magic equipment sell the best magician's silk. It is soft, springy and compressible. An astonishing amount of it can be tucked away into a small space. One square yard can go into your closed hand! In manipulating silks it is desirable to use a fan rather than a wand. You thus weave a colorful and oriental atmosphere into your program.

Silk From an Empty Pocket

Here is a trick you can do without practice. Show your right hand front trouser pocket to be empty beyond any possibility of a doubt. Insert your empty hand into the pocket and produce a large silk handkerchief. Now for the secret. Your trouser pockets have a "dead corner" which can't be seen when the pocket is turned inside out (Fig. 2). This is known to magicians. In the upper left hand corner of the right pocket there is an area in which you can conceal a tightly-packed silk kerchief. Show the pocket empty by turning it inside out and saying, "My pocket has been like this for years — nothing in it but a seam." Tuck it back with your palm toward the audience. Snap your fingers, showing your hand empty, then slowly develop the silk. Allow the pocket to be examined if you care to — there is nothing to conceal after the silk is produced. You can do the same stunt with a dollar bill. This trick is also good for reproducing a duplicate silk previously vanished.

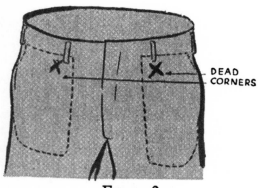

DEAD
CORNERS

FIGURE 2

The Palm Vanish

Use a small silk, not over a foot square. Hold it with one end between your palms, the silk hanging down below the hands. Rub the palms together with a circular motion, gradually taking in more and more of the silk until it becomes a small ball. Face left and palm this off in your right palm, closing the left hand, and pointing at it carelessly with the right. Pick up your fan with the right hand from a table on your left. Simultaneously, drop the silk on your servante, or behind another silk. Tap the closed left fist with the fan, and behold, the silk has vanished! If at first you have trouble palming the silk, just hold it in the right palm with the third finger of that hand. Now — make a duplicate silk appear elsewhere, an apparent transposition.

The Pocket Vanish

Proceed as in the palming vanish described previously. Hold the left hand high and leave the rolled-up silk actually in it. Fumble with your right hand in your right trouser pocket. This will look suspicious. Then smile and show the silk actually in your left. Repeat; but this time palm off the silk in your right hand and put this hand in the pocket. Tuck the silk into the dead corner. Say "No, folks, it isn't here,"

16

and show the pocket empty. Later, vanish the silk from the closed left hand.

The Elastic Handkerchief

Borrow a large breast-pocket handkerchief. Catch the silk at two diagonal corners, about three inches from the actual corners. Gather up secretly several inches of the silk with each hand. Hold the hands well apart, and swing the nearer (right) hand loosely in a circle, winding the silk into a sort of rope. Now give a pull, as if you were stretching it, and remark, "This handkerchief seems to be made of rubber." As you pull, let out a little of the slack that you have secretly taken in. Keep up this rolling and pulling until all the slack is gone. At this point it will seem as though you had really stretched the thing to about twice its normal length. Continue to pretend to roll and stretch the "rope" of silk, using the natural stretch of the silk, but taking care not to injure it. You will be surprised at the apparent stretch of the silk. This is so because the diagonal distance across a rectangle is larger than is generally realized. The added trick of letting out the slack heightens the effect.

The Broken Match

This is an old and easy parlor trick. Place a match under your handkerchief and ask one of your friends to break it. This he does, but when you give the handkerchief a shake, an unbroken match tumbles onto the table, whereupon you say, "There — I knew you couldn't break it!"

The secret lies in having another match hidden in the border of your handkerchief. It is this match which you put in the center of the handkerchief, and offer your victim to break, meanwhile keeping the other match to one side where he will not feel it.

The Vanished Knot

This little parlor trick, though easy, is hard to describe. Take a silk handkerchief and tie the opposite corners together, using a "granny" knot which slips out. Here's how it is done: Put the left end behind the right, bring it toward you and completely around the right. Put the same left end (now the right) in front of the right, wind the former left all around the former right (Fig. 3). Now if you pull the original right, it will become completely straight and slip out of the rest of the knot (Fig. 4).

FIGURE 3

Conceal this fact. Tighten up both ends of the knot all you can. Offer the ends to others to pull, but retain hold of the knot, so that their pulling is to no avail. Hold the slipping part in your right hand with thumb and forefinger on the knot. As you cover the knot with the center of the handkerchief, pull out the sliding part and at the same time wrap the rest of the knot tightly in the center of the handkerchief. Offer it to a spectator to feel how tightly it is tied. Now have some one blow on it — shake it out and show that it has been untied. Compliment your assistant on his powerful breath.

The Dancing Handkerchief

Call attention to a rather large silk handkerchief which lies on your table, or if you wish borrow one from the audience, saying, "I should like to borrow a large, clean handkerchief." In one corner of this tie a good-sized knot. Upon command the handkerchief rises from the table of its own accord and dances in time to the music. It stands up, crawls out of a hat, and answers questions by bobbing its "head."

This is a "thread trick." Black thread is invisible when a few feet away from the audience. Tie the silk around a black

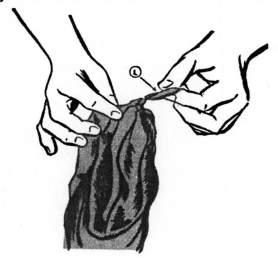

FIGURE 4

thread that extends horizontally across the platform. This thread is attached to the wall or to a chair at one end, and is held by an offstage assistant at the other end. As the assistant tightens the thread, the silk does stunts. This is much more effective in action than as described. At the close of the trick your assistant makes the silk jump as high as possible. You then catch it and take it to the audience for inspection. The assistant lets go his end of the thread, and as you walk into the audience the thread is pulled through and out of the handkerchief.

Magic Knots

Hold a piece of silk in your right hand. Give it a snap. Behold, you have tied a knot in it. This is quite easy. Use a very large (36 inch) silk handkerchief. Hold it in your right hand, rather high, palm facing the audience. The long end is in front of your three large fingers, but back of your little finger. The short end (not much shorter) falls down behind the hand. It is this short end that you must catch and hold onto. Turn the hand, palm down, at the same time giving a sharp swing back. This should enable you to grasp the short end between the right forefinger and middle finger. Hold this tightly, and snap off the loop of silk that surrounds your hand. The result will be a nice knot in the middle of the silk. With practice the whole procedure resolves into a back swing, a snap — and a mysterious knot.

The *"Is Knot"* is another amusing one. Tie the common overhand knot over and over again, very slowly — but when the ends are pulled the knot has vanished. Here's how it is done. Hold an end in each hand. Place the right end over the left. As you do this, nip this right end between the first and

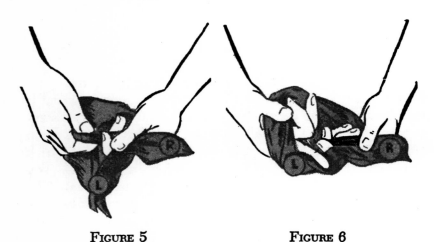

FIGURE 5   FIGURE 6

20

second fingers of your left hand where the silk falls naturally (Fig. 5). Remember — don't let go! Now with your free right hand reach over the far side of the right portion, reach up under it, and grasp the left end with your right finger tips, pulling it through with a rather fast motion (Fig. 6). This is the natural way to tie the knot. However the trick lies in the fact that you hang on with your left forefinger and middle finger, not the left thumb. This releases one end, and the result is a knot that "Is Knot."

Goldin's Color Change

This is a quick color effect that may be introduced into any silk act. The silk may be bought at any of the magic supply houses. The effect requires no practice. Two silks, tied together are made to change color in a very pretty manner, by merely passing the hand over them. There are really three silks, the middle one being a sort of bag sewed to the other two. It is lined on one side with one color, and on the other side with another. As you slide this bag of silk from one silk on to the other, it reverses, the effect being an actual color change.

Production From a Wand

The silk is rolled up tightly on the end of your wand and held under the right arm, the silk concealed. Your sleeves are rolled up. Carelessly call attention to your empty hands. Now take the wand with your left hand and as you pull it out from under your arm, cover the silk with your right hand and hold the wand in it.

Point to the empty left hand with the wand. As you do this, take the wand in your left hand pulling the silk off with the right, immediately turning the right hand with its back to the audience. Strike the right hand with the wand and slowly develop the silk. If it is well done, this is very effective. You may now vanish this silk, or use it for another routine.

Flash Silk Production

The hands are shown empty, front and back. At once a large silk appears in your hand. Obtain a different effect by reversing the routine, the silk growing smaller and smaller, until it vanishes, altogether.

For this trick an artificial celluloid finger is used which is held between the first and second fingers. This "feke" is hollow, and contains the silk. You show the hands empty, waving them about somewhat, so that the extra finger is not noticed. If the audience is at a distance, the illusion is perfect. Now bring your hands together, reverse the finger and slowly develop the silk.

For the vanish, proceed in reverse order showing your hands empty after the silk has vanished. Get rid of the "feke" as you pick up some object needed in your next trick. You may prefer to reach in your trouser pocket and leave the "feke" there, but reproduce the same silk at once from this pocket.

Silk and Billiard Ball Change

For this experiment you have on your left table a billiard ball, a wire standard holding a small cone of flashpaper, and a lighted candle. On your right table you have a handkerchief.

The billiard ball is hollow (a rubber one will do). It has a one-inch hole in it. It has also a loop of horsehair about an inch and a half long, so that a thumb may be slipped into this loop.

Show the cone and place it in the little wire holder. This holder is a ring of wire, set in a standard. Now, get your thumb into the horsehair loop as you pick up the ball with your right hand. Drop the ball into the cone, and turn your hand so that its back is toward the audience. The loop picks up the ball, bringing it into your palm. Hold it there with the second finger and turn to the right, the right hand still back to the audience. Pick up the silk, and with a waving motion work it into the hollow ball; at the same time remove your thumb from the loop. As soon as the silk is in the ball, the hand still in motion, pick up the candle with your left hand, and touch it to the cone. The ball will apparently go with a flash, and the silk will have been replaced by the ball. Now quickly produce a duplicate silk from a slit in your elbow, or from inside your collar.

The "20th Century" Silks

This is a beautiful little experiment in silk, not hard to perform. A red silk with green corners is shown, also two all-green silks. The green ones are tied together and placed in a glass which is not covered. The red one is vanished, and upon shaking out the two green ones, the red is found to be tied between them.

FIGURE 7

The texture of the silk is fairly heavy. One of the green ones is folded diagonally and sewed nearly all around. A duplicate red silk is tied to the end of this green silk, and tucked down inside it with a green corner peeping out. To this the second green silk is tied. A pin is stuck through the hidden red silk to keep it from pulling out accidentally. As you place the two green silks into the glass you pull out the pin and drop it onto the table. Now a good yank will pull out the hidden red silk and show it between the other two (Fig. 7).

The rest of the presentation is routine. Vanish the red one any way you like — wand, fan, flashpaper, pull or what have you. Then "discover" the wandering silk between the others. Applause! See your magic dealer for the latest type used.

Color Changing Effect — "The Dyeing Silks"

An old but good experiment is the silk color change in the paper tube. Roll up a paper tube, pass your wand through it, then poke three white silks into one end. They come out red, white and blue. Next pass these in again. They come out a large flag of tri-color silk. The paper tube is then shown empty.

This requires a "feke" in the shape of a cardboard or metal cylinder in which there is a loose cloth pocket or piece of tape containing in one side the three colored silks and the flag. The other side of the pocket is empty. This gadget lies on the table to your left, under the silks. Show the paper, both sides, then drop this over the "feke" in one motion with your right hand, as you pick up the silks with your left. Hang the silks over your arm. When you pick up the paper you pick up the "feke," wrapping the paper around it loosely. Now pass your wand through the tube, passing it behind the "feke." Snap a rubber band around the paper and poke the three white silks in, one at a time. As you do this, you naturally push out the three colored ones. Push these through the same end in which you put the white ones. The flag will appear. While you are taking out the flag, tip the tube vertically to let the "feke" drop into an open trap in your table, or into a chair-back servante. You may hang your flag over the back of a chair, and tip the "feke" into a servante fastened onto the back of this chair. Show your paper tube empty — tear it in two. Now dramatically, throw the pieces to the audience.

The Crystal Casket

In performing a series of silk manipulations call attention to a small glass casket that rests on a table or pedestal. Wrap a small silk in a piece of paper, which you ignite. The paper and silk vanish in a flash, and instantly the silk is visible in the casket.

Use magic flash paper for this vanish. Roll the silk into a ball, "palm off," and drop it on your servante, or into a small trap in your table, as you pick up the flash paper. Roll the paper into a cone and *pretend* to put the silk into it. When you light the paper it will vanish. You can toss it into the air, which you have time to do, since magic flash paper is not instantaneously hot.

The silk in the casket is a duplicate, retained at the margin or bottom of the device. It appears when the magician or an assistant pulls a thread. This casket may also be used for the production of a large spring ball that completely fills it. If you "force" a color you can seemingly pass into the casket any silk selected.

Production from Clothing

For a comic effect you can produce vanished silks quickly from various parts of your anatomy, the elbow, neck, knee, etc. These are duplicate silks concealed under the clothing, the end coming out through a slit, and attached to tiny black beads, covered with the same fabric as your suit. The production from an empty pocket has already been described in this chapter.

The Stilwell Ball Production

The Stilwell ball is a hollow metal ball painted flesh-color. It may be bought at any magic supply house, or you can make one by cutting a hole in a rubber ball. The ball should be about an inch and three-quarters in diameter, and covered with shellac. Pack into this as many silks as it will hold, all in varying bright colors. Loop the outside end of each into the inside end of the next, so that they come out readily, with a little "tail" to get hold of, one by one.

After producing your first silk from the wand, you can get the Stilwell ball from your pocket into your left hand when you put the wand down on a table at your left. You have the visible silk in your right. Still facing to the left, place one end of the visible silk in your left hand between forefinger and thumb. Of course, the back of your left hand is toward the audience, the hand held high, since you have the ball in it (Fig. 8). Now stroke the silk with the right hand, starting at the extreme top. Do this once, then, as you repeat, merely put your forefinger in front of the silk, the rest of your hand being back of it. At the same time, turn your left hand over and drop the ball into your right. This will not be seen, as it will be behind the silk. Now stroke the silk several times with the right hand, which contains the palmed ball (Fig. 9). Note the position of the hole. Get it just at the top by manipulating with the left hand, as the two hands meet. Your empty left hand now has its palm toward the audience. As the hands come together grasp the first silk inside the ball with the left fingers, and as the right strikes downward, the silk will suddenly appear against the color of the original silk. The effect will be very pretty. Produce the others as rapidly or as slowly as you like. It is easy to show the right hand empty by passing the ball into the left as the hands meet. Practice this "change-over" before a mirror until you master it. The illustration gives a rear view of the move.

To get rid of the empty ball, merely lay the silks on your

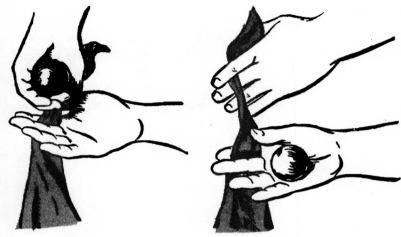

FIGURE 8   FIGURE 9

table and drop the ball on a servante or into a trap, or you can tuck the silks into your right coat pocket, ball and all. Do a knot tying trick with one of the silks, then put the silks aside, leaving the ball in your pocket. Figure out for yourself a way to "lose" this ball — that's what a real magician does.

Silk Production in a Glass

An empty drinking glass is placed on a nickel-plated pedestal about 18 inches high. The glass is covered with a dark handkerchief. Upon raising the covering, the glass contains a red handkerchief.

This trick depends upon apparatus. The pedestal has a hollow space on top large enough to hold the red silk. A cloth cover is nearly around the circle. You can thus show that there is no hole in the top of the pedestal. The thing works with a plunger that you push up with your right thumb. The glass has no bottom. When the plunger is pushed up, the red silk slips into the glass (Fig. 10). All magic supply dealers sell this neat and inexpensive gadget. It's really worth having.

27

The Mirror Glass Production

The mirror glass is perfect for producing a silk. The glass is hexagonal or fluted in shape, and a mirror across the middle gives the appearance of emptiness. The silk is tucked in before hand under the mirror (Fig. 11). When you cover the glass with another dark silk you merely turn the glass around — and behold! A production. Use this glass also to apparently

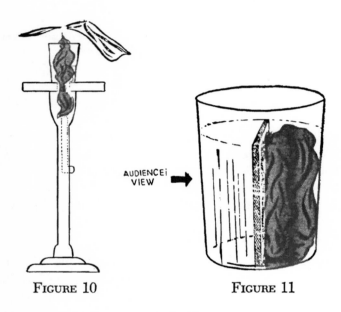

AUDIENCE
VIEW

FIGURE 10   FIGURE 11

change the color of a handkerchief. Start with one silk under the mirror — and visibly place another in front. This device may be obtained at all magic dealers.

The Dove Pan Production

The dove pan is a very old but effective piece of apparatus. The pan may be used to produce anything from a duck to a dollar's worth of Christmas candy; it is particularly good for

28

producing doves, flags and silks. Some alcohol in the pan is set afire, and the fire is extinguished by putting the cover on. This cover is then removed, and the pan is full of whatever-you-like.

The "load" of silken material to be produced is in the cover. When the cover goes on, the "load" goes into the pan. One amusing production is a string of silk baby clothes on a clothes-line; it always gets a laugh.

You can produce as many pretty flags from the pan as the thing will hold. Some magicians have the flags strung on a long cord, with the ends lying outside the pan in the hands of assistants. When the pan is opened the assistants pull the two ends and make a sort of clothesline of flags and banners all across the platform. In handling flags, remember these rules: Never put anything down on a flag; never use a flag as a table drape; the union should be hung correctly, with stars on the flag's right. What's worth doing at all, is worth doing properly. On such a "line" our own American flag should be in the center, and larger than the others.

The Vanishing Silk

We have studied many methods of producing silks. Now we shall consider various ways of making them vanish. A very common device is the "pull" or vanisher. This is a metal tube, painted black, and closed at one end. The closed end is pointed and has attached to it a black elastic cord (Fig. 12). This

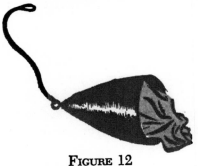

FIGURE 12

cord is passed around the waist, with the vanisher hanging out of sight under your coat. The straps which hold your belt are good stopping points for this "pull." If one strap is too far front, use another, further back. Let us assume that your "pull" is on the right side, hanging under your coat, a little below waist height.

Pick up your silk with your left hand from a table at your right — or make some other excuse to turn to the right. That gives you a chance to get the "pull" in your right hand. Now turn quickly to the left and work the silk slowly into the "pull" with your right hand, then with both hands, meanwhile passing your hands up and down rather quickly. At the down swing, as soon as the silk is inside the "pull" let it go. It will pop out of sight like lightning. Now don't stop the motion of your hands, but keep going a bit longer, turning to face the audience, and bringing the hands well away from the body. This conveys the idea that you still have the silk, and that it can't be slipped under your coat. Roll the imaginary silk into one hand, and throw it into the air or vanish between the tips of your fingers. Show both hands empty. Caution: beware of a watch in the right watch pocket of your trousers. If the "pull" hits this you will hear a noise like a Chinese gong, and it won't help the watch any, either.

A Flash Paper Silk Vanish

Roll a silk into a ball, wind a rubber band around it, and wrap it in a piece of magician's flash paper. Place this on the end of a wire spike that stands on your table. Touch a lighted candle to it and the silk is gone in a flash.

As you pick up the paper from your table on the right, you seem to put the ball of silk into it and begin to wrap it. Actually, you drop the silk into a trap or servante under cover of the paper. The rest is easy, and you are all set to produce your silk in duplicate, elsewhere.

It need not be emphasized that you never do a vanish, or the production of a single silk alone. The two are worked together, so as to present a finished effect. You apparently vanish a silk from one place, and produce it again elsewhere. Thus, you show an empty glass on a pedestal, previously described, wrap a silk in flash paper, vanish it, and pass it into the empty glass. Or produce a flag from your wand, vanish it with a "pull" and produce it immediately from your knee. Create your own effects and develop your own combinations. With several productions and several vanishes you have the foundation for an attractive routine with silk.

The Wand Vanish

Show an empty paper tube and a slender glass vase. Place the tube in the vase and cover the top of the vase with a silk. Now push the silk down into the paper tube with your wand, not touching it with your hands. Snap your fingers! It has vanished! Show the paper tube. Tear it in two. Pass the vase for examination.

This vase is an ordinary "5 and 10" product. The paper is innocent, but it must be very sturdy and tough. The wand is the guilty object — it is hollow. One tip comes off, and to this tip is attached a slender stick, practically as long as the wand. You show the paper tube empty by passing the wand through it, leaving the tip and the stick therein. Later, as you poke the silk into the tube, push it around this stick, into the hollow wand, which comes out and is placed innocently on the table, or used apparently to pass the vanished silk elsewhere.

It is wise to work this trick in combination with the bottomless glass production on the pedestal. Here is a good order to follow:

1. Set up the empty glass on a pedestal and cover it. Push plunger up.
2. Show the paper tube and vase. Push the silk into the paper tube.
3. Show that the silk has travelled into the glass.

4. "Oh no! The silk is not in the paper." Tear the paper in half.

This final tearing of the paper is quite effective. The entire wand vanish may be done without touching the silk with the hands. Even placing the silk on top of the vase can be done with the wand.

The Drumhead Tube

A simple metal tube is examined, then sealed at both ends by members of the audience. This is done by clipping sheets of tissue paper over the ends. The paper on the tube is now broken, and a quantity of silks are produced from it.

The original sealing is "on the level" in every way. Metal rings are slipped over the ends, holding the tissue paper down (Fig. 13C). But there is a small pointed "feke" (B) on the table beneath a handkerchief (A). As the sealed tube is stood up for a second, under cover of this silk, the "feke" is forced through the tissue, in the instant that you pick up the silk. The "feke" is a tube full of silk. The lower end of the "feke" is sealed with tissue, just like the original seal, and cannot be detected. (See your dealer.)

Use the silk on the table for vanishing purposes — and then find (a duplicate) inside the tube. The effect is very pretty. The drumhead tube has special values as the starter for a large production of silk. It can be obtained from magic dealers and comes in different sizes.

You can improvise a drumhead tube with colored plastic cups obtainable at the "5 and 10." Seal a tissue paper cover over a cup with a rubber band. The "feke" is a smaller cup (or one cut down) on which a similar paper cover is glued. The "feke" contains a "load of silk." Proceed as described above.

The Phantom Tube

Present a large metal tube which appears to be empty, and seal both ends with tissue paper held by flat metal rings. A

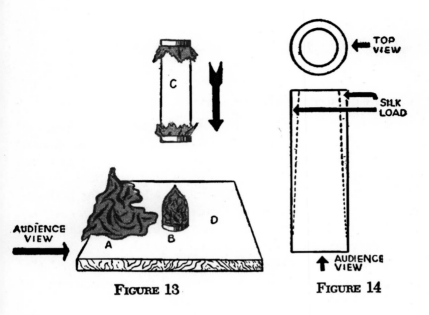

FIGURE 13   FIGURE 14

light is flashed through from the performer's end of the tube
and the audience is certain that the tube is empty. The tissue
paper is now broken and a production of silk is made.

Dealers sell this unusual device. The larger sizes are preferable. This tube has an inner shell, or cylinder, smaller at one
end than at the other. The sketch makes this clear (Fig. 14).
The inside is pitch black. Show the audience the large unfaked
end. They are convinced that all is fair. After sealing, juggle
the tube around a bit so that the spectators will forget which
end is which. The silk is produced from the "loaded" end,
after breaking the paper.

With a little care you can construct this device from a large
cardboard mailing tube. Secure the tissue paper on the ends
with rubber bands.

CHAPTER THREE

MAGIC WITH CARDS

The Popularity of Card Tricks

Card tricks have always been popular with audiences, and many effective tricks are easy to present. For this reason card tricks remain a source of continuous study and practice on the part of magicians. The combinations and possibilities are endless. Cards selected and shuffled by members of the audience are mysteriously discovered. Cards diminish in size, rise from the deck in defiance of the law of gravity and, unlike the leopard, seem visibly to change their spots!

Over the years, a complete literature of card manipulation has been published. Indeed, an excellent "encyclopedia" of card tricks has recently been produced.

Card magic will appeal to the beginner because many striking and novel tricks may be performed with very little practice.

On the other hand, the more difficult branches of card manipulation will afford the expert ample opportunity to demonstrate his skill.

Varieties of Cards

There is a place in magic for marked cards, for mechanical cards, and for decks specially treated. Some of these "trick decks" will be described later. At the start, however, we recommend the use of ordinary bridge-size cards. If your hands are very small, a deck of "junior-size" cards will be more desirable.

As a general rule, cheap cards are preferable to expensive, stiff, or linen-backed cards. For back-palming, fancy card fans, and similar manipulation, it is recommended that you consult a good magic dealer.

First let us consider a few simple card tricks that do not require too much skill or practice.

Finding a Chosen Card

Observe the bottom card of a deck; let us assume it is the ace of spades. Place the deck on the table and ask some one to cut it in as many small piles as he desires. At the same time keep your eye on the pile in which the ace is the bottom card.

Let someone select any card in any pile, and place it on top of that pile or any other. Then have him place all the packets together in any order he wishes. While he is doing this, casually pick up the pile which contains the ace, and put it on the card he has selected, suggesting: "Pile the cards up in any order you like."

If he should place his card on the very same pile you are watching — the one containing the ace of spades, cut that pile in two, saying, "Make as many more piles as you like." Then proceed as above.

Have your helper cut the deck as many times as he desires — straight cuts. Then look through the deck and find the selected card. Merely remember that the ace of spades was placed on top of the selected card. Don't be concerned about the number of times your assistant cuts the deck. It does not affect the result. A straight cut almost never separates the two cards in which you are interested. If it should, one of these cards will be on top, the other on the bottom.

Mind Reading Mystery

Begin by noting the next-to-the-bottom card of the deck. Assume that it is the queen of clubs. Present the pack to someone and ask that person to cut the cards, discarding the upper part. Then ask him to count the lower half, one card at a time, onto a table. Having done this, the top and bottom cards are to be discarded.

Now ask him to look at the top card and to remember it.

You say, "Concentrate on your card. It was a black card. . . . It was a court card. . . . It was a queen. . . . It was the queen of clubs." If you get across the "mind reading" idea, it will prove quite effective.

This is the explanation: When he counts the lower half of the deck, he reverses the cards, which leaves the original next-to-the-bottom card the second card from the top. When the top and bottom cards are discarded the queen remains on top.

Perhaps a better way of discoverng the queen is to permit your assistant to shuffle this card into one of the packets, giving the packet to you. Fan this packet, face toward you, ostensibly looking for the card. When it is located, cut the deck, so there will be nine cards above it, and place this packet face down on the table. Explain, "Well, I missed it — let's try the mental method." Spread the other unused packet face up on the table. Hold the wrist of your helper, and pretend to count his pulse-beats. Remove a black card from the spreadout packet, observing, "This tells me it was a black card." Remove a queen, stating, "This tells me it was a queen." Remove any ten, saying, "And this card — tells me where your card is located — tenth from the top." Have him look for it himself. He will find the queen to be the tenth card from the top as you predicted.

The Transparent Cards

Explain that the cards are transparent only to you, and that you can see through the deck and read a selected card. First get a small piece of silver paper or tinfoil, and paste it on the upper left corner of any card. Place this card second from the top. Offer the deck for a card to be selected, being careful not to show the prepared card.

As the card is returned, hold the deck vertically at the height of your eyes, making a wide fan with the cards. Take the chosen card in your right hand and slide it from right to left of the deck, requesting, "Please tell me where to put it in the deck — anywhere at all." As you do this, the index of the card will be reflected in the bit of silver paper and you can read it. Put the card in, and then, after looking carefully at the deck in order to "see through it" you are able to name the card. This trick can be repeated, and will even deceive experts who are not in on the mystery. Remember that the index will be bottom side up, and that a nine will look like a six. To perform this with a borrowed deck, merely attach your tinfoil temporarily to this deck, using magician's wax.

The Story of the Four Brothers

Take the four jacks, and place one card on top of them. Fan these and show them as the four jacks only. Place them on top of the deck and say, "Once upon a time there were four brothers who were so fond of each other that they held a re-union every year. One of these brothers lived in China." (Put the indifferent top card in the lower third of the deck). "Another lived in India." (Put a jack on the bottom). "The one who lived in India went to South America on a business trip." (Pretend to place the jack already on the bottom into the deck at about the upper third, but actually slip it back with your left forefinger, and take the next-to-the-bottom card instead). "Not knowing this, a third brother went to visit his brother in India." (Move another jack from the top to the bottom). "But when I went to visit the last remaining brother right here"—(in your home town) "I found them all together." Cut the deck several times, making sure no jacks are on the bottom when you are through cutting. It is unlikely that they will be, but if so, cut again and spread the deck face up on the table. The four jacks will now be found together.

Reading the Entire Deck

Turn the top card face up and hold the deck with this card facing your audience. It will naturally appear to be the bottom card. Name this to them, at the same time noting the card that faces you. Put the deck behind you and transfer the card you have just noted to the "audience" side of the deck. Name this also, after a little hesitation, at the same time noting the next one. You can keep this up until the whole deck is named one by one. This is more effective if you can do it blindfolded, managing to read the bottom index of the cards as they face you, by peeping under the blindfold.

Strippers

These are "trick cards." They are a little wider at one end than at the other, and you can feel this difference quite easily. There are a number of amazing tricks possible with these cards.

Distribute a card (or several cards). Now merely reverse the deck, end for end, while your assistant is looking at his card, then replace it. Find it while holding the deck behind your back. You will be able to feel the projecting edges and readily draw out the desired card.

Separate the black and red cards into two piles; reverse one color and riffle shuffle the whole deck. Now you will be able to cut red or black at will; the reds will all cut at one end of the deck, and the blacks at the other. You can draw the cards apart, holding the two ends, and you will have all red cards in one hand and all black cards in the other.

Strippers don't require much skill, and you can have a lot of fun with them. Many of the so called "magic cards" sold by dealers are strippers. They are well worth the money.

SOME BASIC SLEIGHTS WITH CARDS
How to Palm a Card

Hold the deck in your left hand. In order to palm off the top card, place your right hand over the deck as if to square it, your thumb held loosely at your end of the deck, the other fingers held at the audience end of the deck. Your left thumb pushes the top card a little to the right. Your right little finger presses down on this projecting corner, thus tilting the top card

FIGURE 15

into your right palm (Fig. 15). This tilting action is aided by raising the audience end of the deck. Hold your right hand naturally curved, and the card will be retained in the palm.

To Palm Off a Definite Number of Cards

Hold the deck as explained above. Tap the upper few cards toward you, using your right fingers for this purpose. This will cause these top cards to slant at an angle toward you. Now it is quite easy to count the top cards: one, two, three, etc., by raising them with the right thumb. This is called "thumb-counting." Insert your left little finger under the required number of cards, and by raising this little finger, and also the audience end of the deck, the required number of cards are quite easily palmed off. Of course this sleight is covered by the right hand.

Making the "Pass"

The "pass" with cards (Fig. 16) is a method of secretly cutting the deck so that a selected card may be brought at once

FIGURE 16

from the middle to the top or bottom of the deck. There are many different passes with cards, some with one hand and others with both hands. The most common one is done as follows:

As the card is being replaced in the deck, hold your hands *well away from you,* at arm's length. This is important, for it gives you more space for a swing, and more time in which to execute the pass. Most beginners try to make the pass with the hands stationary, and close to the body. It is practically impossible to do this unobserved. On the other hand, with a bit of a swing, I defy the average observer to see the pass when done by an expert.

Place the little finger of the left hand over the selected card and close the deck. The second and third fingers of the left hand are above the deck, the left thumb in its natural position at the left of the deck, and the left forefinger curled up under the deck, out of the way.

Grasp the *lower* half of the deck (which I shall call L) firmly with your right finger tips, pressing it firmly to the left into the crook of the left thumb. Keep up this pressure all the time. The right thumb is at your end of the deck, and the right fingers are at the audience end. The right forefinger doesn't do anything. Now raise the *upper* portion (U) by pushing up with your little finger, and steadying with your next

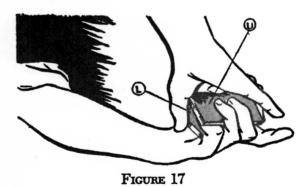

FIGURE 17

40

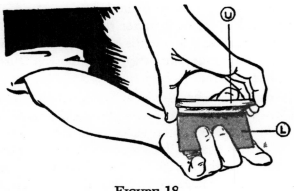

FIGURE 18

two fingers. Gripped (Fig. 17) between the little left finger and the second and third, you pull (U) up and to the right away from (L). At the same time shove (L) into the crook of your left thumb and tip the right side of it sharply upward so that the edges of the two portions clear each other (Fig. 18), and the two packets blend into a complete deck (Fig. 19). When this is accompanied by a swing toward your body it is very hard to see, because the right hand partially covers it.

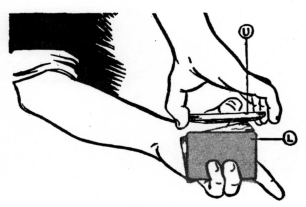

FIGURE 19

If you wish to bring a card to the bottom instead of to the top, put your little left finger under the selected card instead of over it. By counting a few cards above or below your little finger you can bring the card two from the top, three from the bottom, or as desired.

The pass was once considered a basic sleight. It was believed that to be clever with cards you simply must learn it. However, there are now a number of good substitutes for the pass. Learning the pass will be good experience for you in handling cards. Practice it with half a deck before a mirror, and use junior-size cards if necessary. A bridge-size deck is better than a full-size one for this sleight. It helps a lot to say, just before you make the pass, "Are you *sure* you know what your card was?" While your helper ponders and hesitates, you have made the pass.

For the "Charlier" or one-hand pass, see Fig. 20.

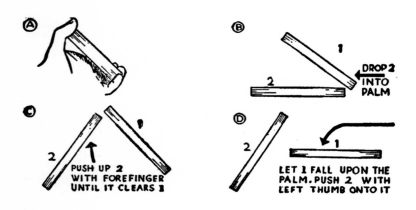

FIGURE 20

42

Naming a Selected Card Without Seeing It

This is rather a false title, for you do see the card, but nobody knows it. You make the pass, or otherwise bring the selected card to the bottom. Pull up your sleeve, getting a glimpse of the bottom card. Now after heavy concentration, you name the card — or you can shuffle it to the top and "find" it in some other way, naming it just before you show it. This gives you an extra climax, always effective.

Substitutes for the Pass

The purpose of the pass is to get control of a previously

BREAK

FIGURE 21

selected card. Remember therefore, that any method that accomplishes this end is worth while. Try these, and use the one you prefer:

1. Insert your little left finger above the selected card, under cover of the right hand. Undercut all the cards below this "break." Throw these cards on top. The selected card is now on top (Fig. 21). Follow with a fast false cut as follows: Cut off the lower half of the cards with your right hand, and slap these onto the deck at least one inch away from you (overhanging toward the audience). Cut off quickly the lower packet and throw it on top. The overhang will make this easy. This fake cut is covered by the right hand.

2. Distribute a card freely and then close the deck. Undercut half the cards and extend the lower packet, having the selected card placed thereon. Throw the rest of the deck from your right hand onto the selected card, but at the same time

insert your left little finger above the selected card. Swing to the right, holding the cards face to audience, gasping all the cards above the "break" with your right fingers and thumb. Deliberately shuffle off all these upper cards, the faces of the cards to the audience. The top card will now be the selected one. This move may be repeated several times, with the result that you will easily collect on the top of the deck several selected cards, in readiness for the rising card trick, or any other effect requiring control of several cards.

3. Use a wide card. To make one, simply paste or wax one card about 1/16 of an inch to the right of another. Have this wide card near the center of the deck, but don't allow it to be taken out. Cut the deck at the wide card, and have the selected card (or cards) put in below it. The audience may freely cut the deck, still you can quickly cut to the selected card. Several cards may thus be controlled, brought to the top, and then revealed to your audience.

4. Crimp (bend down) the near right-hand corner of any card in the center of the deck, as you hold the cards fanned out in both hands, while your helper looks at his selected card. This crimp is made between your little left finger and your third finger tip, which presses down on the card. The selected card is returned just above the crimped one. You can easily cut to this crimp with your right thumb, as you shuffle, leaving the selected card on top. If you crimp the selected card, the audience may actually shuffle the deck and still you can find the card. Don't make the crimp too obvious.

False Shuffles

It is necessary to be able to shuffle a card to the top or bottom of the deck and keep it there, also to apparently shuffle the deck and really not shuffle it at all. Perhaps the most common real shuffle is the ordinary "throw-off" (Fig. 22). The cards are held in the right hand, and tossed off the bottom half of the deck, a few at a time, into the left hand.

44

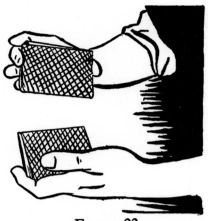

FIGURE 22

How to Keep a Card on Top

Pick up the bottom half of the deck in your right hand. Now toss one batch of these cards into your left hand, but this first lot must be tossed a little to the far side of the former top card, which makes a "break" or overlap above this top card. This is called the "out jog." The next batch will be a bit toward you, and all the others tossed off naturally in the regular manner. Now reach down and pick off in your right hand all the lower packet below the out jog, with your card on top. Toss this packet on top of the cards in your left hand.

Another way is to use the ordinary riffle, where you bring the cards together after cutting the deck in two. Merely make sure that your card (the top one) comes out on top. Several cards may be kept on top or on bottom in this way.

How to Keep a Card on the Bottom

The deck is in your left hand with your selected card on the bottom. Pick off the bottom portion of the deck, all but your card, which is retained by the fingers of the left hand. Then

45

shuffle them in the regular manner, always keeping your card on the bottom with the fingers of the left hand. Or you can merely shuffle with the "top stock" or upper part of the deck (Fig. 23).

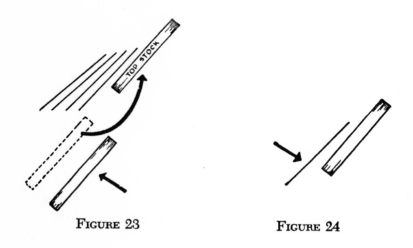

FIGURE 23   FIGURE 24

The riffle method is also good. Simply make certain that the first card riffled down is yours.

How to Bring a Card from the Bottom to the Top

Pick off the lower half of the deck including your card. Shuffle a few cards at a time, down to the last card, which goes on top. This will be your card. Throw off the cards in small lots. The left thumb aids in this shuffle.

How to Bring Your Card from Top to Bottom

Your right hand quickly slides off the whole deck, except the top card, which is retained by the left thumb (Fig. 24). Instantly throw the cards back a few at a time into the left hand, leaving your card reposing comfortably on the bottom.

46

A False Shuffle for the Entire Deck

This is a tricky and deceptive three-way shuffle, known to some magicians. We shall designate three portions of the deck 1, 2 and 3. The shuffle is done by splitting the deck into thirds (packets No. 1, No. 2 and No. 3 respectively) and seemingly shuffling these portions thoroughly. The deck is held as for an ordinary throw-off shuffle.

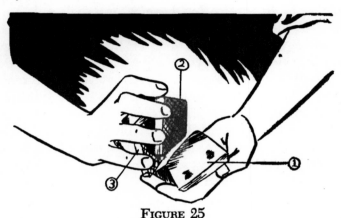

FIGURE 25

In the usual manner take about two-thirds off from the lower part of the deck, leaving packet No. 1 in your left hand. Prepare to toss packet No. 2 back into your left hand. Toss half of the cards in your right hand (packet No. 2) back into your left hand, on top of No. 1: At the same time grip the lower packet (No. 1), still in your left hand, between the roof of the right thumb and right little finger (Fig. 25). Lift this rear packet (No. 1) out and throw it on top of No. 2, which you flop back with your left thumb. Now throw the remaining third (No. 3) back of all the rest, flopping the cards forward with the fingers of the left hand. Repeat as often as you like. This sleight sounds much harder than it really is. The shuffle does not alter a single card in the deck; every card remains in exactly the same position as at the start.

Methods of "Forcing" Cards

It often happens that you will want to make someone take one or more particular cards. There are many methods of forcing. You should have several of these literally, at your finger tips.

The conventional sleight of hand method of forcing is hard to beat. Spread the cards fan-wise, and keep your eye on the card you want to force. You have it, we shall say, on the bottom. You make a pass, or a cut, and bring it to the middle, where you hold it with your left little finger and spread it slightly into view. Just as your helper's hands reach the deck, spread the deck a little more, and see that your card reaches his fingers. It's a matter of timing, and is really quite easy. Don't be hurried; don't present the card too soon or too obviously. If he takes the card, keep on offering the deck for a moment. If you fail to force a card don't let that bother you — simply force it on somebody else. You can easily locate the one you failed to force, and display it at your leisure.

"Forcing decks" are sometimes used. They consist of decks with all the cards alike, so that your victim has no choice — he simply has to take a forced card. "Forcing decks" have their place in magic, but you should not need to use them.

FIGURE 26

There is an ingenious "forcing deck" sold by dealers which has every other card alike, such as tens of hearts. These tens of hearts are shaved off so they are short. Riffle the cards, showing the cards to be all different, for your thumb doesn't hit the tens of heart — but only the honest cards. As you riffle, lower the deck and have your helper insert a finger anywhere. No matter where he does this — he gets a ten of hearts. If you must force one card, this is an excellent sure-fire method, and it looks 100% fair. This is called the Menetekel Deck.

"The slip" or "glide" is a simple forcing method for beginners. Your card is on the bottom. You hold the deck in your right hand, palm upward, thumb on the right side, fingers on the left, forefinger underneath. Poke a few cards an inch or so toward you with your left hand, saying, "Please stop me at any time." As you say this, slide the bottom card toward you with the right forefinger (Fig. 26). When they stop you, take out all the cards below the designated point with your left hand and discard them, except your card, which is kept with the upper deck and shown to the audience as the card they have selected.

FIGURE 27

Making a Fan (One Hand Method)

Let's assume that you have some cards palmed in your right hand, and want to make a nice fan as you produce them. Here is one practical way to do it: Straighten out the curve of your hand, holding the cards by the first joints of the fingers (Fig. 27). Poke the thumb down between the deck and your palm as far as you can, and then, with a sweeping motion, push the thumb away from you, fanning out the cards against the four fingers (Fig. 28). Most of the motion is made by the

FIGURE 28

thumb. The fingers merely hold the cards, and help to spread the fan at the inner edge. If you rub each card in a deck with ordinary stearate of zinc powder, you can make beautiful fans with a mere twist of the wrist.

Stealing Cards from the Deck

This leads to some spectacular card sleights. The face of the cards is changed frequently and visibly at will, and fans of cards are produced from the air or from any place you desire.

To start this routine, face left, the deck held in the left hand with the wide edges of the cards upward, face toward the audience. The left thumb is on top, the forefinger at the extreme left end, and the other three fingers support the deck underneath. You will note that the left forefinger is in a position to poke cards off the back into the right hand. That is the foundation of this series of sleights (Fig. 29).

Stroke the deck with the finger tips of your right hand, from left to right, the thumb going behind the deck. As you do this, poke off a few cards with the left forefinger into the crotch of

FIGURE 29

the right thumb. With a slow, vertical motion, leave some of these on the face of the deck and it will appear that you have changed the front card. Repeat, leaving a different card each time. You can make several changes with each batch of cards stolen from the back of the deck.

Vary these changes with the production of fans of cards. Produce these from the back of your left hand, from under the left elbow, from below the knees, or from the air. This "steal" and its uses require careful study before a mirror. "The steal" is capable of many variations and is worth practicing. It is a

FIGURE 30   FIGURE 31

good method of palming cards, and may be used, as explained elsewhere in this chapter, to change an undesignated card to one selected.

Backpalming of Cards

This is distinctly advanced work in the art of sleight of hand, but for the benefit of those who are never satisfied until they master a subject, I shall describe this backpalming. You will need a pack of cheap, thin cards.

Hold a card in the right hand between the thumb and the curled-in first joints of the middle fingers (Fig. 30). Crook the outer fingers around the card, bending it back as you do this (Fig. 31). Now, holding all fingers firmly together, open your hand wide (Fig. 32). The card has travelled to the back of

FIGURE 32   FIGURE 33

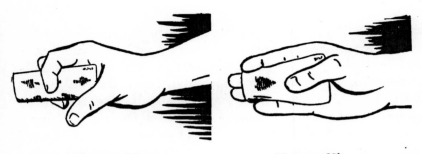

FIGURE 34   FIGURE 35

your hand. To bring it to the front, at the same time showing the back empty, just swing your hand downward and back so that it is vertical, the fingers pointing down. Bend the fingers — and card — into the hand as at the starting position. Grip the card with the thumb against the first joints of the two middle fingers (Fig. 33), then quickly open the hand, keeping the fingers together, still holding the card with the thumb (Fig. 34). The card will now be on the front of the hand (Fig. 35), which can be turned over to show the back of it empty. This whole transfer is done with a circular swing down to the back, and then up and forward, ending with the back of the hand toward the audience (Fig. 36).

To return the card to the back, bring the hand sharply back-

FIGURE 36

ward, then toward you, turn over, and to the front. As you make this swinging motion, push the card with the ball of the thumb, doubling the fingers under and gripping the other end of the card. Now, when you open your hand, the card is on the back. This takes practice, and should be done before a mirror. A wide swing of the arm will conceal the "shift" at first. Later you can do this with a very short swing. This sleight can be done with a number of cards, but for beginners this is quite difficult (Fig. 37). Try it with a few cards, but don't expect to master this effect without considerable practice.

How to Reveal Selected Cards

We come now to the real thrill of card manipulation — the tense moment when the magician mysteriously reveals the cards freely selected by the audience. The cards may appear in an empty envelope, they may rise from a glass goblet, or float through the air into the magician's hands. They materialize at the points of a star, from behind a chair, or at the tip of his wand. The methods of revealing selected cards are legion. Let us confine ourselves to finales that we can present with ease, that are beautiful, often startling, and difficult to detect. One general rule should be remembered — request your assistant to name his card before you reveal it. This greatly heightens the climax.

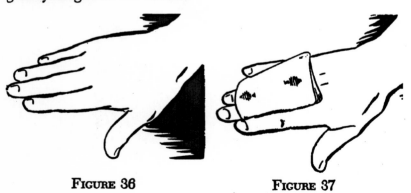

FIGURE 36   FIGURE 37

From Milbourne Christopher Collection

Above: Cardini, the modern master of pantomimic sleight of hand with cards, cigarettes and billiard balls. This Welsh-born wizard has achieved fame as the greatest manipulator of his day.

Milbourne Christopher, a widely televised "hocus pocuser" produces a house of cards below. Has appeared on the Garry Moore, Arthur Godfrey and Steve Allen shows, as well as for the President of the United States.

Any Number from the Top

Make the pass, or otherwise bring the selected card to the top. Start by saying, "Please give me any number from one to twenty." When the number is given, count off the cards onto the table, one at a time, until you get the required number. Then show the top card, asking, "Is this your card?" The audience will say "No!" Gather up the counted cards and put them back on top of the deck, remarking, "I know—I forgot to snap my fingers. I'll try it again." Note that the card is now actually the right number in the deck, for as you counted you reversed the cards, leaving the former top one just where you wanted it to be.

Now have your helper do the counting himself. Snap your fingers just as he gets to the required number, ask him to name his card, and then turn it over. It will be the one originally selected.

It Jumps Out of a Hat

When the selected card is brought to the top of the deck,

FIGURE 38   FIGURE 39

execute a false shuffle and place the cards in a felt hat. In doing this, secretly separate the top card from the others and place it, edge up, in one of the deep hollows of the hat. Snap this place smartly with your fingers from below the hat. The card will leap out, making a very pretty and surprising finale (Fig. 38).

The Turn-Over

Bring the selected card to the top of the deck. Now drop the deck on a table and the selected card mysteriously appears, turned face upward. The trick is a simple one. Just slide the top card an inch sideways as you are about to drop the deck. When the cards fall, the air will turn the top card over (Fig. 39).

It's Wrong Side Up

While your helper is looking at his selected card, turn the deck bottom up. This will not be noticed if you first reverse the bottom card, so that after you have turned the deck, the back of this reversed card is visible on top. Now have the selected card shoved in anywhere, being careful not to open the deck up. Once more turn the deck over under cover of your hand, and execute a very quick riffle which will not show the selected card to be wrong side up.

Now say, "Please tell us the name of your card." When this is done, supposing the card to be the ten of clubs, exclaim "Ten of Clubs, turn over." As you say this, give the pack a loud snap, and spread the cards backs up in a fan-shaped half-circle on a table, being careful not to show the bottom card. The ten of clubs will be face up. Pick it up, remarking, "If you catch a pack of cards young enough you can teach it almost anything!"

The Mexican Turnover

The selected card has been brought to the top and palmed

in the right hand. You say, "If I did this trick correctly — and I very seldom do — the card you selected will now be on top." Push the top card about an inch to the right with the left thumb, at the same time turning it face up with the back of the right hand, by merely pushing upward from underneath. This top card, which now lies on the deck face upward, is announced to be the wrong card. Pretend to be surprised, and explain that you snapped the wrong finger, or used the wrong magic word. Repeat the turnover move with the back of the right hand, but this time leave the palmed card on top. Have your assistant name his card aloud. Make a snap and a riffle, and then show this card to be on top.

The Visible Change

After bringing the selected card to the top, hold the deck in the left hand with the long edge upward. Turn left; the faces of the cards are toward the audience. Your thumb is on the upper edge of the cards, your index finger at the left end, and your other three fingers beneath the lower edge of the cards. Pass your right hand lightly across the face card, asking, "Is this the selected card?" Of course you will be told that it isn't. As you pass your hand across the deck, let your right thumb go back of the deck and steal off the selected card (Fig. 29), slipping it into the right hand, where you palm it. Now change your stroking to a vertical motion, and leave the palmed card on the front. It will seem as though the front card has been visibly changed to the selected one. Practice this before a mirror.

Mind Reading

It is necessary to force a card to get this effect. You then explain, "You may suspect me if I ask you to return the selected card to the deck. Therefore, I shall try to name your card by mind reading. Please concentrate on your card. Think! Now show the card to the rest of the audience. Everybody concentrate! It is a red card. Is that right? It is a court card? Thank you. It is a diamond . . . a King of Diamonds!"

Note how much more effective this is than merely telling your audience the name of the card at once. To the audience the result is magical.

Rising Cards

There are many ways to present rising cards. Here are several of the more practical and interesting ones. Some are done purely by sleight of hand — others by means of apparatus.

Thread to Button Method

Attach a fine black thread to a vest button. The thread should be about two feet in length. Put a knot in the end, and then attach to this knot a small pellet of wax. Ordinary "Plastecine" or modeling wax will do, if you mould and soften it. Do not use "magicians' wax." It is too sticky. Attach this wax pellet just under the edge of a lower vest button. Now you are ready. Have several individuals select more cards. As the cards are returned to the deck manage to have them all put back in the same place, using a wide card for this location. A cut will then bring the whole lot to the top. Note that you make the cards rise from the back or top of the deck, so that the *last card returned* will *rise first*. Consequently call on your audience in proper order, the last man to replace his card being called first, and so on.

As you return to the platform, hold the deck high in your left hand, at the same time getting the wax into your right fingers. Now turn your left side to the audience. Hold the deck vertically in the left hand, the back of your hand toward the audience, the left arm extended across the body, well over to the right, waist height. The faces of the cards are toward the audience. As you square up the cards with your right hand, attach the wax to the back card. Hook your right fingers under the thread, place your right hand over the deck,

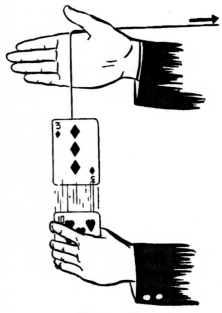

FIGURE 40

wave it about mysteriously, and then raise this hand rather smartly. The back card (after being named by the person who drew it) will rise into your right hand (Fig. 40). Place this first card on the front of the deck. As you do so, your right thumb is on the face of the deck, your fingers on the back of it. Detach the wax with your fingers, stick it on the back card, next to rise. The result will be quite mysterious. You can even have the audience initial their cards, reading the initials as each card rises, thus showing that the selected cards are actually the very ones that rise. For this effect use a dark background and moderate light.

The Spirit Slate

You can make this gadget yourself. Get an ordinary school slate and fit onto one face of it a piece of tin exactly the size of the inner surface of the slate. Paint the tin a dull black color on both sides. When this "feke" is held on the surface of the slate, the latter can be shown on both sides. It appears innocent of writing. Actually you have already written with chalk on one side of the slate the words "Ace of Clubs." This is covered with the black tin and is not seen. Your table should have a black cover.

Force an ace of clubs, and have it shuffled into the deck. Now show the slate to be clean on both sides, and place it, tin side down, on your table. Display a silk handkerchief which has "an audience on one side and nothing on the other." Pick up the slate, leaving the tin "feke" on the table. Cover the slate with the silk, holding it with the blank side facing the audience. Explain that you are going to call on the spirits to tell the name of the card. Make a scratching noise with your finger on the slate, and call the spirit by some funny name, asking him to hurry up. Change hands, thus reversing sides and bringing the writing toward the audience. After "stalling" for a minute or two, remove the silk and show the "Ace of Clubs" written on the slate. Thank the spirit, and ask him to "sign off."

Rising from a Card Box

The selected card has been brought to the top. Place the deck in the cardboard box in which it was purchased, but facing toward the rear of the box. This is just opposite to the way we usually insert a deck. As you tuck in the flap of a card, leave the selected card *outside the flap*. Now hold up the box and poke the card upward with the forefinger, at the same time making a waving motion with the hand.

They Rise from a Goblet

This effect depends on threaded cards. The cards that rise are duplicates. Ordinarily the rising is handled by an assistant offstage, who pulls the thread. The effect is wonderful.

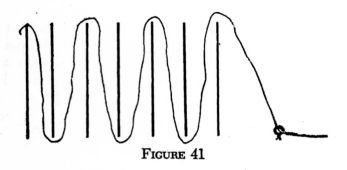

FIGURE 41

To thread cards, cut a slit in the top edge of one card (this one doesn't rise) and slip the end of a thread into this slit, a knot keeping it from pulling out. Thread it below the *last card* to rise, above an indifferent card, under the next-to-last card to rise, above an indifferent card, under the first to rise (if you use three cards) and over an indifferent card (Fig. 41). Put this packet of threaded cards face up on your table under a silk, where it won't be seen. The end of the thread goes through a ring on the table, then off stage to Jake, your husky assistant.

Force three cards and have someone shuffle them freely into the deck. As you return to your table, place the deck face up on top of the threaded cards. At the same time pick up the silk (used to screen the threaded cards) and polish the goblet, showing it to be ordinary. Now shuffle the deck lightly, the threaded cards being kept out of the shuffle. Place all the cards in the goblet, the threaded ones being located in the middle.

Here, with all due solemnity and ceremony, have the cards named by the takers, one at a time, telling them to order the cards to rise. As Jake pulls the thread, the cards rise on order.

An amusing bit of by-play occurs when a card "fails" to rise. Ask the taker what it was. He replies "The Queen of Spades." You retort, "Aha, that accounts for it — you can't order a Queen about like that. You have to be *polite* to a Queen. We must *request* her to rise. Queen of Spades, rises!

Another stunt is to have a card come up the audience. You shove it back into the deck come up properly. This it does. Of course yo cate card threaded, back to the audience, and to shove it into the unthreaded portion of attaching the end of the thread to your wand yo with Jake by simply moving forward. Phonogra sometimes adapted for card rising, a pulley b which to wind up the thread.

Rising from the Hand

The card or cards are on the top of the pack cards vertically by the fingertips of the right han of the deck to the audience. Poke the cards slow the forefinger, with a waving motion of the dec

Another excellent method is to raise them with little finger. Stand with your left side to the audien the deck vertically in the left hand, the back of the the audience, the arm across your body, and well tov right. The front of the cards face the audience as usu the top edge of the deck a few times, with right fo

FIGURE 42

right, little finger actually slides the card up, but it will
ar to be rising by some magnetic power exerted by the
inger (Fig. 42). The card is taken between the right
b and forefinger after it has risen to about two-thirds of
eight. Try this before a mirror — it's fun.

ds from Back of a Chair

his is a mechanical device consisting of three clips to hold
ee cards, and a revolving rod held by a spring catch.
en a thread is pulled the rod revolves and the three cards
p into a vertical position. Of course you force three dupli-
e cards. This device may be attached back of anything.
can be purchased from any magic dealer.

he Card Star

Master magicians, for several decades have used the card
ar to produce selected cards. Most dealers have it in stock.
his metal star is set up on a standard, and the cards are
ttached to clips which fold back into the center of the star.
When a thread is pulled, the outside card is released, and the
springs snap out all the others. They seem to come from
nowhere onto the points of the star. As in all such tricks,
duplicate cards are previously forced.

CHAPTER FOUR

MAGIC WITH COINS —
FOR THOSE WHO HAVE THEM

How to Palm a Coin

Palming is the foundation of all sleight of hand. You can readily learn how to palm a coin of any size from a dime to a half-dollar. Magicians use the half-dollar size almost exclusively, because it is just the right width for back palming. To start with, why not try palming a penny?

First sensitize your palm by scraping it with the edge of a coin. Now press the coin as hard as you can into the palm of your right hand, making a little indentation. Lower the ball of your thumb onto it a little, and try to hold it in the palm. Continue pressing the coin into the palm. Shortly, you should acquire the ability to hold it there by a gentle muscular pressure exerted by the ball of the thumb. Still, your hand will appear to be open (Fig. 43).

Always carry a coin in your right coat pocket. Practice pressing the coin into your palm with your two middle fingers — retaining it there while you open the hand fairly wide. If you drop the coin, it only takes a second to retrieve it and start anew. Soon you will be able to hold the coin balanced on the tips of your two middle fingers. Press it quickly into the palm, and hold it there without losing it. When you have learned this, and can use the hand naturally with a small object palmed, you have made a long stride in the art of sleight of hand.

When you have a coin palmed in your hand, don't hold the hand open stiffly. This attracts attention. Simply hold it half-closed, in a natural manner (Fig. 44). If you desire to call indirect attention to its being seemingly empty, make use of

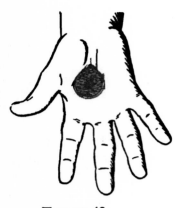

FIGURE 43   FIGURE 44

the hand for some apparently good reason. Pull up your sleeve, or point to the other hand where the coin is supposed to be, or pick up your wand or other object employed in the trick you are presenting. Your audience will then assume that your hand must be empty. Do not say it is empty. Let the audience decide this for itself.

Producing a Palmed Coin

To produce a palmed coin, simply reach down back of one knee, or under your vest, letting the coin slide to the tips of your fingers.

Coin Passes

In magic terminology a "pass" means pretending to place an object in one hand, when actually it is retained in the other. There are several good passes with coins that should be mastered. Assuming that you have been practicing coin palming, you should be able to snap a coin from the tips of your fingers into your palm and retain it there, while using the hand naturally.

66

The Palm Pass

This pass is done by palming. Hold the coin between the right thumb and the tips of the two middle fingers, as if you were going to place it in the left hand with a tossing motion. Now, as you swing your hand upward and to the right, press the coin into your palm with the two middle fingers, then swing the hand down and appear to place it in your left hand which closes instantly. Face toward the left, pointing with the right hand to the closed left. Pull up your left sleeve, thus indicating that the right hand is empty. Vanish the coin from your left hand with a rubbing motion and a toss into the air. Now, nonchalantly produce the coin from wherever you like. Practice this before a mirror, first, actually tossing the coin into the left hand, then executing the pass, so that you can't tell by sight which one you do. Remember, this pass *must be done smoothly and naturally*. It isn't especially rapid, but rather a gentle toss which seems entirely innocent and simple.

The French Drop Pass

This will merit careful study, especially since you will employ it in billiard ball tricks. Hold the coin between your right thumb and forefinger, your palm being horizontal and

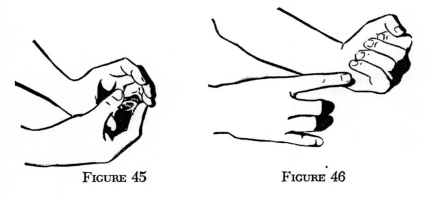

| FIGURE 45 | FIGURE 46 |

upward. Bring your hands together, the right remaining as described, the left palm down. Tuck the left thumb under the coin, pressing the left little finger and outside edge of the palm against the tips of your right fingers (Fig. 45). This conceals the coin from your audience for a few seconds. At this point drop the coin into your right hand and instantly separate the hands widely. Turn toward the left at once. The right hand is turned palm toward you, the coin in the palm concealed by pressure of the fingers. This hand assumes a pointing position as in the palm pass (Fig. 46). The left hand is closed as if holding the coin.

The Wrist Drop Pass

Hold the coin between the right forefinger and thumb. Pull up your right sleeve with the left hand. Now push up the back of the left sleeve with your right wrist as if you were trying to raise the sleeve. As your right hand passes the left *on its way back,* drop the coin onto the left hand which is palm downward and bent way back to receive it at the finger tips (Fig. 47). The left hand executes a catching motion, the whole pass being performed too quickly for the eye to follow. Advance the closed right hand as if it still contained the coin. Do a vanish from your right hand and produce it with your left hand as you desire. Practice this before a mirror. It is very deceptive if executed smoothly.

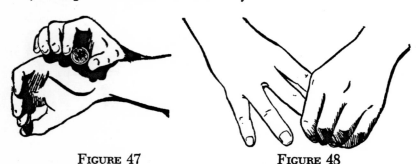

FIGURE 47   FIGURE 48

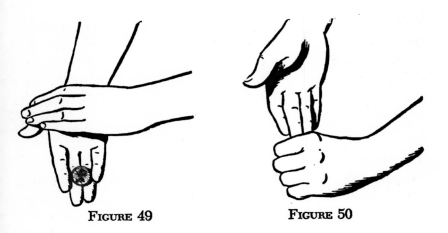

FIGURE 49   FIGURE 50

The Throw Pass

Pretend to throw the coin from your right finger tips into your left hand. Actually you palm it in your right hand (Fig. 48).

The Back Palm Pass

This is an excellent move, but it calls for a high degree of skill. The coin is held flat on the right fingers, the edges pinched between the two outer fingers of the hand (Fig. 49). When the left hand conceals the coin for a moment in the sliding-off motion of taking it, the coin is backpalmed with the right (Fig. 50). It vanishes from the open right hand, and the audience assumes that it was taken by the left. A more detailed description of back-palming with coins will be described further on in this chapter.

The "Clink" Pass

Spread several coins (quarters or half-dollars) on your right hand from palm to finger tips. Make a tossing motion, pretending to pass these into your left, turning the right hand over and reversing the coins, so that they make a distinct jingle. As you turn the hand, let the coins fall onto the finger tips of the right hand, retaining them there secretly. Close the left hand as though the coins had actually been passed. Hold the coins in the right hand with the center fingers. Be sure that they do not make any noise. Pretend to throw the coins through your knees, and produce them with a loud clinking noise in your right hand. The illusion is perfect, if properly executed.

The Vanishing Coin

Execute the palm pass, pretending to hold the coin in the left fist, at about shoulder level. Now say, "Please somebody hold my wrist firmly, like this — so that the coin can't escape." Suiting the action to the word, grasp your left wrist as if you were demonstrating how to do it. At this moment drop the coin from your right hand into the left sleeve. The volunteer following your example will hold the wrist, and certainly will be surprised when you open both your hands and explain, "Money is awfully hard to keep."

The Hooked Coin

Dealers in magic supplies sell a half-dollar with a tiny needle-pointed hook on it. Make this coin disappear by any of the passes you have perfected. While you make the motions to produce it from behind knee or elbow, hook the coin out of sight. The result is a perfect vanish. The combinations with this device are many. Work them out for yourself.

The Jumping Coin

A half-dollar is tossed into a tumbler. Suddenly it starts to jump and leap about inside the glass. If anyone in your audience questions you about its activity, the coin answers by doing a number of jumps. This effect is quite startling because the coin makes a loud, jingling noise as it hops about. Finally it leaps out of the glass. All this may be done with a borrowed and marked coin.

70

The secret lies in a length of fine black thread, one end of which has a bit of wax and lies on your table. Your assistant who is off-stage has the other end of the thread. When you place the coin on the table and call attention to the glass press the coin into the wax. Your assistant does the rest.

This trick may be greatly improved by placing a glass cover over a tumbler. A small coaster will do, or a piece of plate glass weighed down by any small object. For this variation, file a notch in the edge of the tumbler through which the thread will run. Let the thread come up through a screw-eye on the table near the glass.

The Dissolving Half-Dollar

Borrow a half-dollar. Mark it and place it inside a handkerchief. Your assistant — anyone from the audience who offered the coin — is asked to hold this coin, distinctly seen within the handkerchief. He is now asked to drop the coin (under cover of the handkerchief) into the glass of water. The audience can hear the coin drop into the water. Now reach into your helper's pocket and produce the marked coin. Ask him to remove the handkerchief from the glass. All are surprised to see that the coin has disappeared.

A disc of glass, just the size of a half-dollar will give you

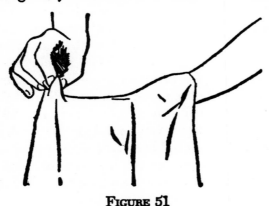

FIGURE 51

FIGURE 52

the means of performing this little trick. Palm the coin in the act of putting it inside the handkerchief, substituting the disc of glass, which you have held from the start of the trick.

Passing a Coin Through a Handkerchief

Place a coin between the left thumb and forefinger, palm turned upward. Drop a handkerchief over the hand, and take hold of the coin through the handkerchief with your right forefinger and thumb (Fig. 51). Turn the coin over toward you, and again grasp it with your left forefinger and thumb. This will wrap the coin into a fold of the handkerchief. At the same time explain, "I want you to be absolutely sure that the coin is really in the handkerchief — look!" Reach down and lift up the front bottom hem of the handkerchief, exhibiting the coin, which is still held in your hand (Fig. 52). Then, with a quick motion, throw down not only the front hem, but also the back hem which has been spread over your left wrist. The coin is now really outside the handkerchief, and covered merely by a fold. Give the handkerchief a twist, and ask someone to hold it, while you still grasp the coin. Slowly work the

72

coin out of the fold; it will appear to come right through the fabric. Retain your hold on the handkerchief and take it into your own hand, giving it a shake to conceal the fold. Then show that "there is no hole in it."

Passing a Coin Through Paper

Cut a hole in a piece of paper. The hole should be slightly smaller than a half-dollar. Ask someone to pass a half-dollar through this hole, which of course cannot be done. Fold the paper through the center of the hole, and drop the coin into this fold. You will find that if you bend apart the edges of the paper the coin will drop through.

Passing a Coin Through the Table

Place two coins on the table "as far apart as possible." Pick one up with your left hand and put it under the table. Place the other in the center of the table with your right hand. Suddenly there is a snapping sound — and both coins are found in the hand under the table.

This little after-dinner trick is not difficult to perform. In putting the coins "as far apart as possible" place one on the near edge of the table, just over your lap. Take up the distant one rather ostentatiously with your left hand; at the same time push the near one into your lap with the fingers of the right. Now instantly swing the closed right hand forward, and make small circles with it, the hand apparently holding one of the coins. In the meantime the left hand goes under the table and retrieves the coin from your lap. Bring your left hand under the center of the table and snap one of the coins loudly, as you pretend to press the one in your right hand through the table. Now show the two coins in your left hand, explaining, "Remember, my two hands never approached one another — they were as far apart as possible!" You will be greeted with a chorus of, "Let's see you do that again," but if you are wise you won't.

Eating a Coin

Announce that times are hard, and you have been reduced to eating coins. Sit in a chair and pretend to put the coin into your mouth. Drop it on the floor between your feet, and in bending down to pick it up, reach *under* your right knee; as you bring it up with your right hand, leave it under this knee, quickly carrying your hand to your mouth. Now go through the motions of enjoying your light lunch. The coin seems to have vanished. To retrieve it, slap the outside of your left knee with your left hand, pretending to get the coin from there. While this misdirects attention, get the coin with your right hand and pretend to pass the coin through your left knee into your right hand.

Penny and Dime

Show a penny and a dime in your left hand. Deliberately close the hand, then open it. Behold, the dime is gone. Now produce the dime from below your vest with the right hand. The penny is hollow — merely a shell, just the right size to hold a dime. When you close your fist, the shell slips over the dime which instantly vanishes. This effect is obtainable at any magic dealer's. Of course, you have another dime in your right hand all the time, and merely produce it from wherever you please.

The Chinese Coin

This is one of the prettiest coin tricks imaginable. String a Chinese coin on a cord and cover it with a handkerchief. Now you detach it from the cord, although the two ends are firmly held by a keen-eyed member of the audience.

This calls for two identical Chinese coins. (The trick may be done with rings or washers if Chinese coins are not obtainable.) String the coin on the cord, and cover it with a handkerchief. The ends of the cord are held by a volunteer. So far, so good. Now, with the duplicate coin palmed in your right hand, put your two hands under the handkerchief and ask for plenty of slack. Take a loop of the cord and poke it through your duplicate coin. Run this loop around the coin, and tell your assistant to tighten the cord (Fig. 53). This will hold the duplicate coin on the cord by a sort of loop that makes it detachable, but this is not evident to anyone who sees it. Slide the original coin off toward the left end of the cord under cover or your hand, saying at the same time, "Please remove the handkerchief." When this is done, the assistant will see the duplicate coin attached to the cord, and imagine that it is the original. Now take the cord away from him, saying, "Thank you. I want to see if I have done it correctly." Examine it closely, then hand him the cord so that he will have to grasp

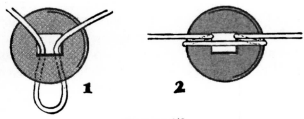

FIGURE 53

it inside your hands, which leaves you holding the original coin, and your helper "holding the bag." Place the handkerchief in your pocket, at the same time leaving the coin there. Now under cover of your left hand remove the coin with your right, and show that you have "actually passed one solid body through another." If carefully done there is simply no solution to this trick. However, it must be practiced.

Back Palming Coins

For your coin, use the half-dollar size, preferably one of the "palming" coins sold by dealers for this purpose. They are quite thin, have sharp edges that will give you a good grip, and are just the right width. Younger people may find quarters too small and half-dollars too large. Try both and do your best to find a coin to suit the size of your hand. "Palming coins" have another advantage — they can't be spent, so that you always have a few coins with which to practice.

The coin is held across the inside ends of your fingers, and you grip the edges of it with the inside tips of your first and little fingers. Bend your two center fingers back and revolve the coin completely around, using as an axis the two points you have gripped by the outer fingers. This places the coin on the back of your hand, still held by the inside tips of the outer fingers. To bring the coin to the front, reverse this process.

At first you will drop the coin every time you try this. Then, as the inside of your finger-tips become more sensitized, you will be able to back palm with a reasonable assurance that the coin won't go rolling off somewhere under the furniture.

Practice this back palming in your right coat pocket. If the coin drops — as it often will — pick it up again and continue practicing. When you get the knack of it you can cause a coin to vanish by holding it in the hand, making a tossing motion, and quickly back palming it. Now show the back of the hand by swinging it in a wide motion to the rear as you front-palm the coin, and turn the back of the hand toward the audience. Repeat this as many times as you wish. To produce the coin, show the front of your hand empty, reach up into the air, and seem to catch money from nowhere. Practice these moves before the mirror. You will be pleased by the startling effects that are produced.

Try to learn back palming with either hand, which you should also do with ordinary palming. When you acquire the ability to back palm coins, you are on the road to becoming a real wizard.

Back Palming Effects

Hold the coin in your right hand down near your knees and appear to place it in the left hand. Really back palm it. Now appear to toss it through the knees into the right hand. Make a tossing motion with the right hand, as you back palm. Pretend to catch it with the left. Don't show it — merely toss the imaginary coin back and show it in the right hand again. Now actually place the coin in the left hand. Pretend to toss it through the knees, but really palm it in your left hand. Appear to catch it with the right, and without showing it, toss it back. Show it actually in the left. By this time your audience is confused, and ready to believe your statement that you "have a wooden leg with a knothole in it." Vary these moves sometimes, by really throwing the coin *back* of the knee and catching it. This is quite easy, and will puzzle any audience. Just bend the knee slightly as you make the throw, and do it very swiftly. This stunt also works well with a billiard ball. These moves at the knee may be done with ordinary palming if you are not skilled in back palming.

Try this "passing through the knees" with two coins, one in each hand, doing back palming with either hand.

The Miser's Dream

A clever magician by the name of T. Nelson Downs, a pioneer in the art of coin manipulation, is famous for performing this trick to perfection. Obtain a handful of magic coins and a derby hat. You may borrow a hat from the audience. You may also use a small, tin pail if you prefer. Some skill in back palming is necessary. Have the coins on your table and get them into your left hand as you take the hat from the table.

The coins are held in a stack in the fingers of your left hand which is pressed against the inside of the hat. The hat is held with the open end up, your thumb being on the outside. Make a catching motion in the air and pretend to throw a coin into the hat, at the same time dropping the lowest coin into the hat from inside. If you prefer, you may start with one coin palmed in the right hand, producing it and showing it to the audience. Pick the first coin out of the hat and show it to the audience. As you seem to toss it into the hat again, back palm it, dropping another stacked coin instead. Now reach into the air and produce another (the same) coin. Pretend to throw this coin into the hat. Each time you do this, drop a coin from the bottom of the concealed stack. This dropping of coins with the left fingers calls for some practice. It should be perfectly timed, and each coin must make a loud clink as it falls.

This can be kept up indefinitely. If you run out of coins in your left hand, just pick up a handful from the hat with the left fingers to show to the audience. When throwing them back, retain a number in that hand and carry on.

Produce coins magically from anywhere: your knees, your elbow, the bottom of the hat, from the air, from anywhere. Pretend to pass one right through the side of the hat, back palming it and dropping a stacked coin inside. You can seem to toss a coin into the air by back palming; now stick out the hat and pretend to catch the invisible coin, which will clink with a comic effect.

At the end, gather up a large handful of coins in your right hand. Use the "clink pass" and seem to pass the whole lot through the knee. Drop them onto a plate with a clatter. Now take a deep bow.

Dealers sell a coin-dropper that may be attached to the inside of a hat. It drops one coin at a time. With this device, the magician can keep his left hand outside the hat. But he must get rid of the gadget when he is through. For beginners the method I have described is simple, yet very effective.

The Coin Wand

For "The Miser's Dream" and other coin productions, magic dealers sell a coin wand that produces coins at its tip as you press a button on the side of the wand. This device is very good as a "flash effect" in any coin act. However, it is merely an accessory, and should be recognized as such.

78

CHAPTER FIVE

MAGIC WITH BILLIARD BALLS

Billiard Ball Manipulation

Sleight of hand with billiard balls is one of the most fascinating branches of magic. There are indeed very few billiard ball tricks that do not require skill. For this reason we must consider the art of billiard ball manipulation from the standpoint of skill acquired only by study and constant practice. We shall start with the simplest of sleights and go gradually to the more complicated manipulations.

You can make billiard balls appear and vanish in the most mysterious manner. You can have them change their color, increase their diameter, multiply in number, and diminish in size until they disappear completely. There are almost no limits to the beautiful and puzzling effects that are possible. The combinations that offer themselves to the capable and original artist are endless.

The Kind of Billiard Balls to Use

Real billiard balls are made of ivory or heavy composition. They are not used by magicians. Dropping a real billiard ball on your foot would be a serious occupational hazard.

Magic billiard balls are made of light wood, and are painted with a soft finish that help them stick to the palm. Avoid celluloid or highly varnished balls. They are liable to slip out of the hand. A ball with too much gloss can be rubbed to a soft finish with powdered pumice stone or a mixture composed of alcohol and laundry cleaner. A rubdown with magician's wax is effective.

The size of the ball should vary according to the performer's hand. A ball an inch and a half in diameter is about right for the beginner. Dealers sell an excellent "golf ball" set, including a metal shell. These are ideal. They are made of sponge rubber, and seem to stick to the fingers. For practice any light spongy, rubber ball is suitable. Magic dealers also list wooden balls, an inch and a half or an inch and three-quarters in diameter, beautifully finished, in various colors.

How to Palm a Ball

It is easier to palm a ball than a coin. The curved surface gives your hand a better grip (Fig. 54). Carry a small ball in

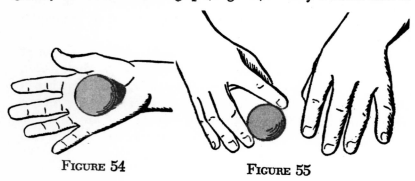

FIGURE 54   FIGURE 55

your pocket. Practice palming, and the art of using the hands while holding a palmed ball. Try writing a letter with a small ball palmed in your hand. Develop skill in palming with either hand, because in billiard ball magic, you *must* be able to use either hand equally well. You should have little trouble in learning to palm a small ball of any diameter. It will help if you sensitize your palms by rubbing them with the edge of a coin.

Passes With Balls

The "French Drop" described in the chapter on coins is an excellent pass with billiard balls. Remember that a hand supposed to be holding a ball should not be closed tightly. Place a ball in your left hand and close your fist. Note how the hand looks. Now remove the ball and make the same kind of fist. You will have to stretch your fingers back toward your wrist. Study this position carefully, and never fail to make the empty hand look exactly like the full one. *Please read these last five sentences again.*

The Finger Throw

The Finger Throw is a handy and natural pass. Hold the ball between the first and second fingers of your right hand, the back of the hand to the audience (Fig. 55). Swing the hand rather widely to the right as if you were going to throw the ball into your left hand. At the same time squeeze the ball into your palm, and with a swift throwing motion appear to place the ball in your left hand. The left hand appears to pull the ball off your right finger tips. The left hand still has its back to the audience, the fingers pointed downward. Close the left and turn the fingers up, making a fist, as if holding the ball.

The Roll-Over Pass

The ball is held in the palm of the right hand, the fingers holding the ball naturally. Place the ball deliberately in the center of the left palm, and roll it between both palms with a clockwise motion. Both hands are held horizontally, the left underneath (Fig. 56). Palm off the ball in your right hand, as you quickly close the left hand and make a fist. This palming is covered by the closing fingers of your left hand.

The Throw Pass

This is just like the finger throw pass, except that the ball is first held naturally in the right hand instead of between the finger tips. It is of course retained in the right palm.

81

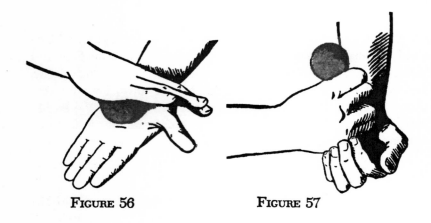

FIGURE 56   FIGURE 57

The Drop Pass

Hold the ball on top of the right closed fist, which is held in front of you, the back of hand to the audience. Open the right hand a bit, and pretend to drop the ball through the right into the left hand. The fingers of the left hand are vertical, and touch the back of the right fist (Fig. 57). Actually the ball is retained in the right palm. The right hand is opened rather widely as the left hand is closed. This is one of the very best passes.

The Fist Pass

The ball is held balanced on top of the right fist, which is held *across the body* and well toward the left side, as you face left (Fig. 58). Now reach around to the right and front of the ball with your left hand, and seem to pick it off the fist. The left hand is held so that the back is to the audience, the thumb pointing down. At the moment when the ball is concealed, let it drop into the right hand, pressing it into the palm (Fig. 59). Open the right hand and point to the closed left fist, which is turned over as if containing the ball. Practice this before a mirror.

82

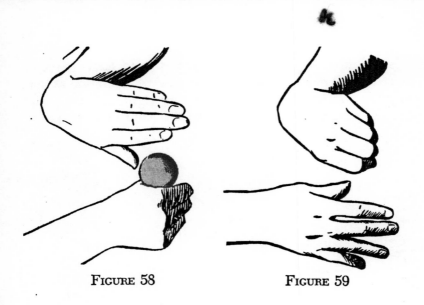

FIGURE 58   FIGURE 59

The Wrist Drop Pass

This pass is described in the chapter on coin manipulation. It may also be performed with a small ball.

Changeovers

Now that you have learned a number of ways to apparently pass a ball from one hand to the other, begin to reverse your practice so that you can execute these passes with either hand, which will give you the required versatility. You will also want to show either hand empty at any time. This is done by means of a "changeover" in which the ball is indetectably passed from hand to hand. You will thus learn to vanish a ball, show both hands empty, and then produce it from some unexpected place.

The Across Body Changeover

The ball is palmed in your right hand, but is apparently held in the left fist. Vanish it with a rubbing motion, showing the left hand empty. Place your right second finger on the base of the left palm at the wrist as if you were pointing at the empty hand (Fig. 60). Now swiftly turn right, rubbing your palms one over the other, transferring the ball to the left palm

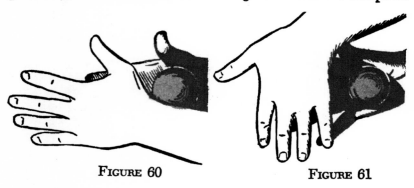

FIGURE 60   FIGURE 61

as the hands pass each other. The position of the hands will now be reversed, the right hand being shown to be actually empty, the left fingers just touching the right wrist. You may repeat this turning of the body and changeover of the ball —but never more than once. There are many changeovers, and using a variety of them is interesting and fascinating.

A good variation is to turn the just-emptied hand, so that its back is to the audience as it passes in front of the body. First, point to the back of the empty hand. Now slowly turn the empty palm toward the audience. This is more effective than showing the empty palm immediately. Use your mirror to learn this.

The Vertical Changeover

This is very deceptive and interesting; if it is varied freely with the Across Body Changeover, you will really puzzle your audience. The empty left hand is held vertically and a little below waist height, the fingers pointing straight down, palm toward the audience. The right hand, holding the ball in its palm, strokes the left palm with the finger tips in an up and

84

down motion (Fig. 61). First stroke the palm downward. Then raise the left hand as if to repeat, pressing the ball into the left palm. Instantly, turn the left hand, its back to the audience and continue the stroking motion down the back of the left hand (Fig. 62). Now your right hand is empty. But don't show the empty palm (Fig. 63).

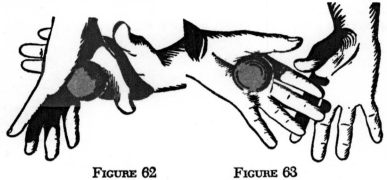

FIGURE 62   FIGURE 63

In the same way, stroke the back of the right hand with your left, to indicate "nothing here." Now, and not before, turn the empty hand over to show it empty. Quickly execute the Across Body Changeover and show the left hand empty too. Produce the ball with your right hand. Repeat this routine in reverse manner. Your audience will be completely astonished. Practice this procedure before a mirror. Practice it over and over again.

The Overhead Changeover

Face left and hold both hands at about the height of your head. The ball is in the right palm, the hand being held vertically, the fingers just touching the left palm (Fig. 64). The left hand is held in a horizontal position, palm toward audience. Stroke the left palm from wrist to finger tips. As you repeat this, press the ball into the left palm and quickly turn the left hand over, continuing to stroke the back of the left hand (Fig. 65). Show the right hand empty. Now when the hands are opposite, turn both hands over simultaneously and take the ball into the right palm. At the same time execute a downward motion with the right hand. This is actually the same as the Vertical Changeover, but is done with the arms at a different angle. It is better for stage audiences, since it is visible from a distance, and is learned with very little practice.

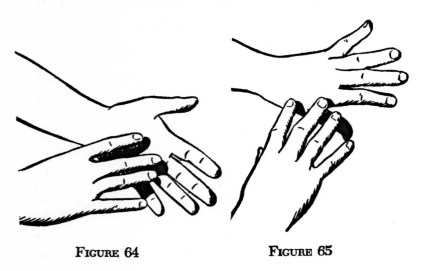

FIGURE 64   FIGURE 65

WHAT HAVE WE ACCOMPLISHED THUS FAR?

If you have devoted a reasonable amount of time to practice and have mastered the moves previously described, you should now be able to do the following sleights: vanish a billiard ball in several ways and show either of the hands empty — reproduce the ball from the air, or from wherever you please. You have also a considerable amount of skill in passes and changeovers. Moreover you possess a feeling of confidence, knowing that you can entertain and astonish an audience with billiard ball sleights.

How to Vanish Billiard Balls

With the use of changeovers you seldom need to really "get away" with a billiard ball. But in case you do, here are some suggestions:

Using any pass you like, vanish the ball from the left hand by tossing it into the air. Face left and pick the ball out of your right knee. Repeat these moves, but this time, you actually take the ball in your left hand. Make a tossing motion with your left hand, with the back of the hand toward the audience, the ball palmed in the hand. Now reach down as before and pretend to produce the ball from your right knee with your right hand. This, my friends, is misdirection. While all eyes are riveted on your right hand, drop the ball into your left coat pocket. Pretend to get the ball with your right hand, seem to pass it into the left, do a fake changeover, and slowly show one hand empty, the other empty, and then show both hands empty at once.

Vanish with Wand or Fan

Make a pass, pretending to place a ball into your left hand. Reach with the right hand for your wand, which is on a table to the left. Drop the palmed ball onto a servante. Now tap the closed left fist with the wand, and show that the ball is gone.

The Sucker Pull

This is a small rubber sucker attached to a length of elastic cord (Fig. 66). This cord is around your waist, under your coat. As you turn right, for some reasonable pretext, grasp the sucker in your right hand. Now, turn sharply left and attach the sucker to the ball, making an up and down motion as you "lose" the ball under your coat. Continue this motion, extending your hands well away from the coat and body. Now vanish the ball after a couple of false changeovers. A little glycerine rubbed into the sucker will improve its effectiveness.

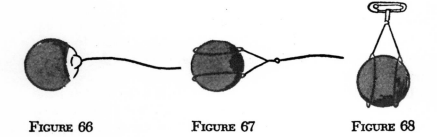

FIGURE 66   FIGURE 67   FIGURE 68

The Clip Pull

Here is a vanishing pull that you can make. It is constructed of wire, and is covered with rubber tubing, cloth, or adhesive tape. The clip consists of two loops or rings of wire parallel to each other. These are the exact size and distance apart to clip a ball and hold it (Fig. 67). Attach this gimmick to an elastic cord — and there you are! Use this as a sucker pull. This clip is also useful when attached to your coat with a safety pin (Fig. 68). It keeps a ball handy for quick production at all times. Some magicians prefer to have these under the vest.

Tables, Clothing and Accessories

Magic tables are serviceable in connection with billiard ball tricks. The servantes are convenient for vanishes, and if you have a small trap in the table (a hole lined with black velvet) you will be able to use this effectively for the same purposes. You may rig up a runway of wire under the front of the table, and use this to get possession of a few billiard balls, one at a time. Use your ingenuity, and see what you can do with the idea.

Some magicians use a vest servante to vanish billiard balls. This is practical for stage work when you are wearing a dress suit or tuxedo. The servante is merely a narrow pocket held open at the top with whalebone. It is placed between the top of your low-cut vest and your shirt-front. Into it you can drop billiard balls or other small objects. If you have lost your boyish figure, the vest servante will hardly be practical.

The billiard ball tube is a convenient accessory. This is a tube of cloth attached to the inside of your coat with the lower end terminating just where your extended hand can reach down and extract a ball. The bottom is closed with a rubber band, or wire clip. You can put several balls into this tube, and have them handy for productions.

The outside lower pockets of your coat are used extensively in ball productions and vanishes. You face right, for example, produce a ball with your left hand — and vanish a ball into your right pocket. With a little practice you can do this undetectably, especially if the pockets are low, and the flaps are tucked in.

The vest is good for the production of a ball, although this takes real skill, for a move toward the bottom of the vest is always rather suspicious. With proper misdirection it is possible to get a ball from under the vest and palm it. Use a wire clip under the vest, otherwise the premature production of a large white ball dropping on the floor may cause you to "lay an egg."

Billiard Ball Stands

Dealers sell attractive stands on which to place the balls you have produced; these dress up an act, for they are very colorful. Some are innocent of trickery; others are mechanical stands which vanish or produce billiard balls. If you build a stand of your own, you can place it in front of a black velvet screen, and back up certain parts of it with velvet, attaching little servantes in back of the stand. It will then serve for some beautiful vanishes and color changes. For example, if you have a white ball on the stand, approach it with a red ball palmed in your hand. Merely tip the white ball onto the servante as you place the red one in its place. The effect will be a mysterious color change.

Other stands have shells in each holder instead of balls (Fig. 69). These tip up and look just like solid balls. As you seem to place a ball on the stand you merely tip up a shell, palming the solid ball to be produced again and again. In this way, the whole stand is filled with "billiard balls," although you really use only one. "It ain't honest."

FIGURE 69

Color Change Effects

Some of the most beautiful sleight of hand effects are produced with color changing billiard balls.

Old fashioned methods include using a ball that is half one color and half another. Still another swindle is based on the idea of palming a shell and placing this onto a ball of another color.

The most effective method, however, is that of pure sleight of hand. The balls are all bona fide, and are cleverly changed one for another, with most interesting results.

Finger Tip Color Change

Let us assume that you have a billiard ball tube on the left side of your coat, and that you intend to do your vanishing into the left coat pocket. Start out with a white ball in your right hand. Make a pass, vanish the ball, and produce it with your right hand at the right knee. As you do this, while facing left, get a red ball from your tube into the left hand. All eyes will be on the right hand, as you produce the white ball. Now bring the hands together and transfer the red ball to the

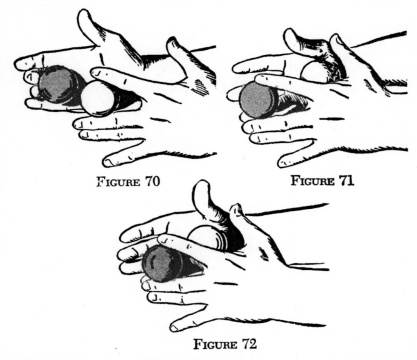

FIGURE 70

FIGURE 71

FIGURE 72

right palm as you visibly place the white one between the left forefinger and middle finger (Fig. 70). Your left hand is palm forward and horizontal. Now you are ready for your first color change. You are still facing left. Stroke the left hand from finger tips to wrist once or twice, and as you move the right hand *away* from your body, draw the red ball completely away from the palm with the tips of the third and fourth fingers of the right hand (Fig. 71). Now, with one motion, palm the white ball in your right hand, and replace it with the red ball (Fig. 72). Push the red ball toward you as it is gripped by the left finger tips. This beautiful effect is much easier to do than to describe. **Try it before your faithful mirror.**

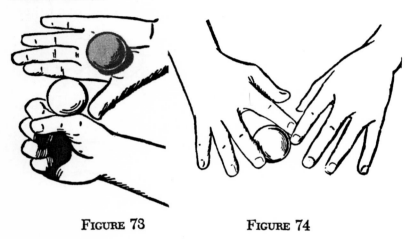

FIGURE 73   FIGURE 74

A Master Color Change Move

Let us assume you have completed the sleight just described. To get rid of the white ball, which is now palmed in your right hand, take the red ball from your left hand with your right forefinger and thumb, at the same time pressing the white ball into the left palm. You are still facing left. Instantly turn the left hand over, back to audience, holding it rather nigh. Place the red ball on your right fist, execute the fist pass, pretend to toss the red ball into the air with the left hand, and as you produce the red ball from the air with your right, drop the white ball into the left coat pocket, and get another colored ball. This color change routine may be continued until several changes have been made. Reverse these moves, using your right pocket and your routine will be very effective.

Other Color Change Methods

1. Appear to drop a white ball through your right fist, which already contains a red ball. Catch the red ball with your left hand, immediately opening the right hand wide, for a second, to show that it is "empty." Of course the white ball is palmed in the right hand. Don't let the two balls click as they approach each other. Try this first with the red ball held in the left hand. This insures silence.

2. Face left. A colored ball is concealed in your left hand. Show a white one on the right fist, as for the Fist Pass (Fig. 73). Cover this with your left hand, as for the Fist Pass, but drop the white one into your right palm leaving the red ball balanced on your fist, in its place. Open the right hand as you take the red ball off the fist.

3. Hold a white ball in your right hand as for the Finger Throw Pass, your left hand holding the palmed red ball, the back of the hand presented to the audience (Fig. 74). Exe-

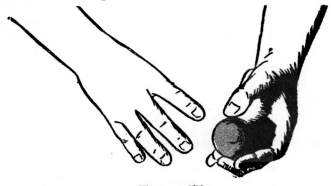

FIGURE 75

cute the Finger Throw Pass, at once showing the red ball in the left hand (Fig. 75). It will appear to have changed color upon striking the left hand.

93

4. Place a red ball in your right coat pocket. Show a white ball; execute a pass into your left hand, and seem to throw the ball with the left hand into the right coat pocket. Reach in with the right hand and get the red ball between your finger tips. As you withdraw your hand, show the white ball in the upper hand, but drop it back into your pocket, withdrawing the red ball (palmed) instead. The hand should be closed. Make another pass without showing the ball. Vanish the supposed white ball, make a few changeovers, and produce the red ball. You have no white one to worry about; it is already disposed of. This is very subtle.

5. Now comes one you yourself are going to invent. Make it the best of the lot.

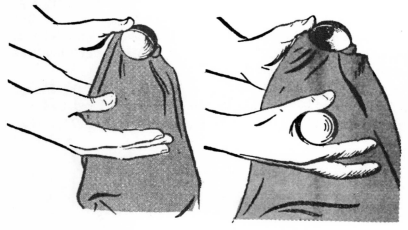

FIGURE 76   FIGURE 77

Ball Through Silk Handkerchief, Shell Method

This is done with one ball and a shell that fits over it. The rubber "golf" balls sold by the dealers are best for this trick. Show the silk hanging down from the first and second fingers of the left hand, at the same time holding the ball and shell in the same hand between finger and thumb, the shell and back of hand toward the audience. Show the ball on all sides.

The right hand is obviously empty. Place it behind the silk (Fig. 76). As you do this loosen the shell and drop the ball out of it into your right hand (Fig. 77). The solid ball is

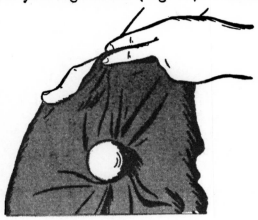

FIGURE 78

will revolve in your hand, since the silk is entirely removed. At this moment the ball will drop into the shell, whereupon you press the ball and shell together, and display it freely. A shell really sticks to a rubber ball, but shells used with wooden balls fit more loosely and are dangerous for this trick.

loosely held in the right palm, fingers curled, the silk covering all. Press the shell onto the ball with your left hand, grasping the shell through the silk with your right hand. Tap it gently, then display the silk from both sides (Fig. 78). It will appear that the ball is half way through the silk. As you display the ball, replace it in your hand with the shell underneath, and lying in your right palm. Loosen the ball from the shell and gently pull the front of the silk, where it hangs down. Your right hand is held horizontally, the fingers curled. The ball

Ball Through Silk Handkerchief, Sleight Method

This is performed exactly the same way as the coin trick and is called "Passing a Coin Through a Handkerchief." It is described in the chapter on coin tricks. You will note that this effect is even more striking with a ball than with a coin. See Figures 79, 80, 81 and 82.

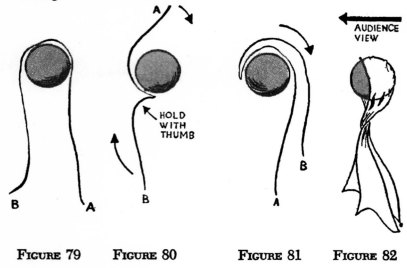

FIGURE 79   FIGURE 80   FIGURE 81   FIGURE 82

Multiplication and Subtraction

Produce a ball. It rapidly multiplies itself until there are four between your finger tips. Now they vanish one by one, until they are all gone — a very pretty effect, capable of endless variations. The rubber "golf ball" outfit is excellent for this effect. It is sold by many dealers. I shall describe a simple way of presenting this trick, and you may amplify it as you wish. No two magicians perform this trick in the same way.

There are three solid balls, also one metal shell which looks, from the front view, like a solid ball. Place the shell in your right trouser pocket, and place two balls in your left coat pocket. One ball (the third) you produce in any way you like. Now make a pass and pretend to throw the ball with your left hand into your right trouser pocket. As you reach into the right pocket, the ball palmed in your right hand, you simply bring the ball and shell out together, showing these as one solid ball. This is an easy way to get possession of the shell. To make the balls multiply, you face left, your right arm held horizontally across the body, back of your hand to the audience. The ball and shell are held between the right fore-finger and thumb, the shell's face to the audience.   Now roll the ball out of the shell with the second finger so that it is held between the first and second fingers. This is the basis of all ball and shell sleights. Learn this sleight with balls between all your fingers. Now at the moment that you apparently produce this second ball in your right hand, you are stealing another ball out of your left side pocket. Reduce the apparent two balls to one, and turn sharply toward the right side (Fig. 83). Keep the balls palmed close to the body. Wave your hand and produce two balls again (Fig. 84). Next take the solid ball from between your right fingers with your left hand, and leave the third ball in the shell (Fig. 85). This is an easy

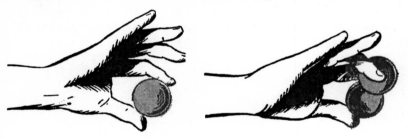

FIGURE 83   FIGURE 84

and natural motion, for you always tap the balls together to show that they are solid. This tapping is done every time you want to get a ball into the shell. You face right to do it. Move the ball to between second and third fingers.

Now, again face left, produce the third ball from the shell, and at the same time get the last one out of your left pocket. All eyes will be focused on your right pocket. Again turn right, tap the balls together, insert the last ball in the shell, and produce this last ball while still facing right (Fig. 86).

To vanish the balls, take a solid ball from the shell each

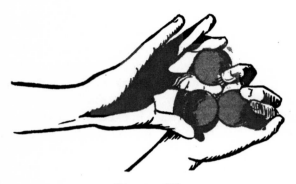

FIGURE 85

time you tap the balls together. Simply reverse the previous process, dropping the extra balls into your left coat pocket as each one is vanished from your right.

FIGURE 86

There are a number of amusing effects which may be presented with this trick. Have a ball inside the shell in your right hand, and a ball in your left hand. Seem to throw the ball into your right elbow (palming it in the left), at the same time bringing the ball out of the shell. Try throwing the ball through your knees in the same manner. Put your wits to work inventing new sleights with the balls and shell. The possibilities are endless.

To get rid of the shell, appear to pass the ball and shell into one of your pockets. As you take the ball out, leave the shell in the pocket. You can vanish the last ball and shell into a servante by using your wand. If you use the rubber "golf ball" outfit, the ball and shell can be manipulated and vanished together.

The Diminishing Ball

Procure several balls ranging in size from one and a half inches in diameter to the size of a marble. Paint them all the same color. You are now ready. The method of causing the big ball to seemingly shrink to a tiny one is the same as described for color changes. Simply substitute, and "squeeze" the ball to a smaller size as each substitution is made. The two smallest balls can be held in the hand at the same time, which speeds up the trick. This effect is always amusing to any audience.

Ball to Streamers

Turn right to pick up a ball from your table, and at the same time get possession of a roll of paper streamers, the same color as the ball. This roll may be taken from under the right side of your vest, or from your right pocket. The roll of ribbon streamers should be small enough to palm easily. At the same time get a "sucker pull" from under the right side of your coat. Turn slightly left, vanish the ball with the pull, and produce the colored streamers. If you attach a lead sinker to the center of the paper roll, it will drop to the floor and the ribbon will fall with a very pretty spiral effect. Hold the sinker in place with a paper strip.

This trick may also be presented with finely cut confetti instead of the streamers. Seal your confetti in a small tissue paper bag. Break the bag and let the confetti fly into the air as you fan it vigorously.

The Rising Ball

For this effect you need a fairly light ball. The ball has a hole in it and runs loosely up and down a rod attached to a pedestal. The ball seems to obey your command and also answers questions — one for yes — two for no. It may be passed for inspection.

A thread is attached to the top of the rod. The ball forces this thread down. When the thread is pulled, the ball naturally rises. The thread may be attached to your wand, or even worked by an assistant. If you prefer, you may have a ring on the rod instead of a ball. In using the wand method, pass a hoop around the pedestal. As you pick the hoop up to show it solid, transfer it from hand to hand. In doing so, you easily manage to pass the wand through the hoop. Now you put the hoop around the pedestal or toss it aside.

The Polychromatic Ball

The audience is given a choice of a number of different colored silks. One having been selected, roll it in your hands; it is changed to a billiard ball, exactly the same color as the selected silk.

The secret lies in the ball which is made of glass. It is hollow and you work the silk into it with a waving motion. The ball is palmed at the start of the trick. The glass will show the colored silk inside, giving the effect of a solid billiard ball. The Abbot Magic Novelty Company of Colon, Michigan, makes a good transparent plastic ball for this purpose.

100

From Milbourne Christopher Collection
A rare photograph of Madam Herrmann, the widow of Alexander Herrmann the Great, performing on one of the most elaborate stage sets ever used in magic. She is seen in the dark costume near the center of the stage, as "Cagliostro" the 18th Century mystic. After the death of her husband at the turn of the century, she toured the country with a show of her own.

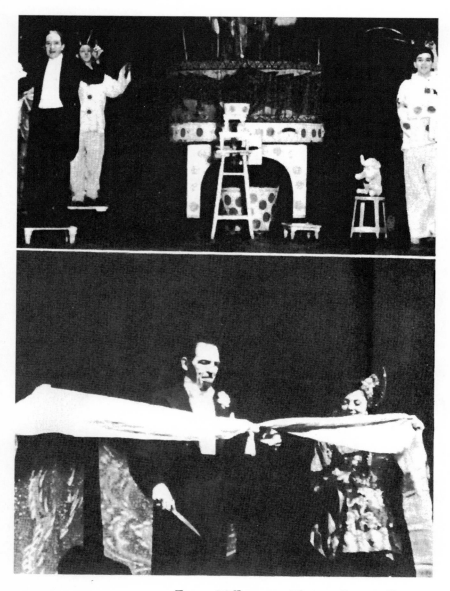

From Milbourne Christopher Collection

Above: Thurston's Chinese Water Fountain illusion. A wave of his wand, and water spouts from the heads of his assistants, their finger tips, and from objects about the stage. Then, a girl floats mysteriously over the magic fountain at the center of the stage.

Below: Jack Gwynne cuts a turban in two, and "hocus pocus"— it's back together again! The Gwynne family performed under the billing, "Oriental and Occidental Oddities."

One of the greatest "Chinese" magicians of all times was Chung Ling Soo. Chung was really an American named William Robinson, who masqueraded as an Oriental wonder worker. He was killed performing the sensational bullet catching trick, March 23, 1918, on the stage of London's Wood Green Empire Theatre. He is shown at extreme right loading a girl into the mouth of a cannon.

From Milbourne Christopher Collection

Marvin Roy performs the modern version of the needle trick. He swallows light bulbs and a cord, then, brings them up neatly strung and lit. Lit bulbs appear and disappear at his finger tips.

Below: Sorcar, the best known magician in India. He performs both the traditional Indian magic and the more up-to-date sorcery of the western world. He is shown below, on a recent trip to Paris, apparently about to make the Eiffel Tower disappear.

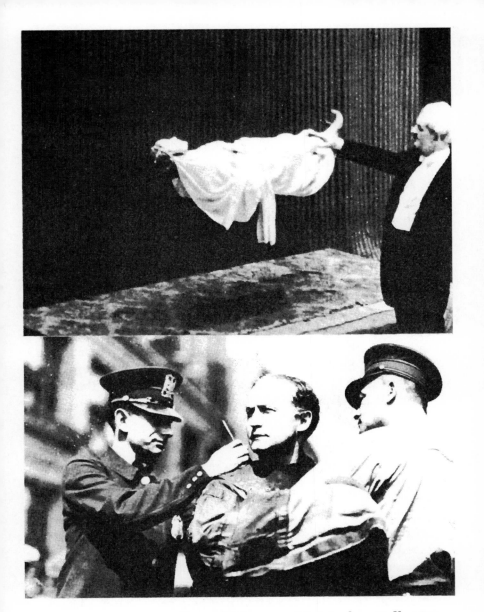

Above: Harry Blackstone, the most famous of modern American illusionists, is shown performing the great levitation trick. The subject floats in thin air at his command.

Below: A rare photograph of Houdini, the great escape artist, being strapped into a strait jacket by policemen. He is then hauled aloft, hung upside down, and makes his escape within a few minutes, while thousands watch.

CHAPTER SIX

MAGIC ACCESSORIES

Magic Accessories

As a magician you will use various equipment and many small pieces of apparatus, some visible, others which your audience will never see — you hope. Such utility items or accessories are used over and over again in many ways. Let us consider some of them.

A Lighted Match From Your Pocket

When you need a match for any trick, simply bring it lighted out of your pocket. This will be quite easy if you attach a square of stiff cardboard covered with fine sand paper inside the pocket. Strike the match as you remove it from the pocket. Dealers have a mechanical device for producing the same effect. It is inexpensive and highly recommended.

The Changing Bag

This is a useful accessory. You may have occasion to change one small object for another. You may want to change a card, selected by the audience, and sealed in an envelope. Perhaps you desire to change a borrowed handkerchief for one of your own, which you may cut or burn, restoring the original later. Possibly you have a number or a color that you wish to force. You may want to cut the necktie of a "stooge" in the audience, restoring it later. For these purposes the changing bag is effective. It consists of a cloth bag on a short wooden handle. The bag is really double, and when you turn a part of the handle, a metal half-circle swings around inside the bag, presenting the inside of a duplicate compartment.

For example, you wish to force the color "red" on your audience in order to perform a silk trick; you already have a duplicate red silk "loaded" for use. Display a number of colored silks and show many small bits of cardboard of different colors. These you drop into the changing bag. Ask a spectator to reach in and take out one cardboard, choosing any that he touches. By this time you have switched the bag so that any cardboard he may touch will be red — they are *all* red. Of course you hold the bag too high for him to see the inside. You have forced the required color. The red silk has been "freely selected," and you go on from there.

Pulls and Holders

Several different types of "pulls" and holding devices, for vanishing or producing silks and billiard balls have been described in the chapters relating to those subjects. Admirable devices for holding and delivering thimbles, coins and even lighted cigarettes are obtainable from magic dealers.

The Magic Funnel

We shall assume that you need a glass of water for your next trick. Here is a good way to produce one. Hand an empty glass to a boy who has volunteered to help you. Ask him to hold it a few inches below his chin. Take an ordinary looking funnel and put the spout above the glass, holding it near the mouth of your helper. As you pump with one of his arms a stream of water spurts from the funnel and fills the glass.

This is a trick funnel. It is double, and its secret compartment is filled with water. All you have to do to start the water running is to remove a bit of adhesive tape that covers a hole in the handle. This admits air, and the water begins to flow.

There is another comical effect with the funnel, one that is sure to get a laugh. It is used in combination with a "foo can" (described later) held on someone's head. It is a screamer.

FIGURE 87

First call two boys forward. Now pour a small glass of water into the can. Place your hand over the mouth of the can, invert it, and place it carefully on the head of one boy. He holds it with his left hand. "Pierce" his left elbow with an awl, and have the other boy pump his right arm. Now by use of the funnel, the water seems to pass from the can through the head, out at the elbow, and into the glass (Fig. 87). These magic awls are available at all dealers. The blade of the awl goes up into the handle. The illusion is perfect. **At the finish,** show that the "foo can" is empty.

The Silk Cabby

Utility apparatus is a term applied to items that have many practical uses. Such an item is Thayer's Silk Cabby. It is one of the best utility items ever devised. This little oriental silk cabinet is about seven inches long, five inches high and four inches wide. The front and back are hinged to the bottom and fall open when desired, showing the cabby empty. These

108

doors are not faked; nothing is attached to them. There is a round hole at each end of the cabby, through which you can poke silks. A good quality 36 inch silk can be concealed or changed inside this seemingly empty box.

Use the Cabby for the 20th Century Silk Effect described in the chapter on silk, or for silk color changes, or for vanishes and productions. I use mine mostly for the cut and restored necktie trick. Simply have a stooge wearing one of your stock neckties, with a duplicate in the cabby. Use him for another trick, then lead him into the necktie trick. Finally restore the tie in the cabby. This is first rate comedy, and will knock your audiences out with laughter.

A Cigar Box Utility Vanisher

Following the line of the famous Jack Gwynne rabbit trick, the writer has made up and often uses a utility vanishing box. The crude hinges are made of adhesive tape secured by tacks. The pocket is black cloth with elastic in the upper seam. Decorations are made by Scotch tape . This will vanish silks up to 36 inches, and may also be used for the production of small items. To use it, simply hold it as shown in the sketch and make a complete revolution toward the audience (Fig. 88). The doors will fly open and the box will appear empty. For a production, show it open as explained above; now reverse the process. Open the unfaked door, and produce the item.

The Impromptu Mirror Glass

The mirror glass is a stock utility item, valuable for transposition and color change routines with silk, rice and other articles. It is simply a fluted glass of good size, with a mirror inserted half way back. It looks empty, even when the rear compartment contains silks. When you cover it with a dark silk and turn it around while moving it from one spot to another, objects may be changed, produced or vanished. You will appreciate its usefulness. It is quite simple to make one

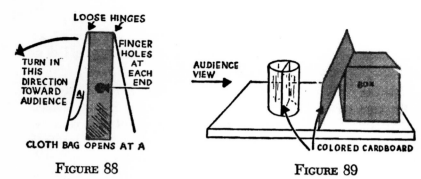

FIGURE 88   FIGURE 89

without any mirror. Get a sheet of Bristol Board, brightly colored on both sides. Insert a well-fitted piece of this cardboard into any fluted glass, holding it with a bit of adhesive tape at the bottom. Lean a larger square of the same cardboard against a box or other apparatus on your table. Place the glass in front of this background, now you are all set (Fig. 89). Beware of lifting this glass until it is safely covered with a dark silk.

The Bottomless Glass — Old and New

If you wish to vanish or steal a lemon, billiard ball, coin, ring or rolled up silk, the bottomless glass is exceptionally handy. The article is placed in the glass; your fingers underneath keep this article safely inside. As you cover the glass with a silk, the article is easily stolen.

However, you can get the same effect with any small, straight glass by means of a simple sleight. Hold the glass in your right hand, a dark silk in your left. As you cover the glass with silk, simply invert the glass (Fig. 90), assisted with your right fingers. Now pick up the glass with your left finger tips, at its top rim. You may even snap a rubber band around this upper rim (actually its bottom). You have of course palmed off the ball or other object in your right hand.

In showing the glass empty, simply reverse the process under cover of taking off the silk.

110

FIGURE 90

The Utility Silk Tube

This slender transparent plastic tube is used for vanishing, producing, or changing the color of silk by means of an invisible mirror device. It is built by the Petrie Lewis Company of New Haven, Connecticut, and is both well made and practical.

The Foo Can

Clever people, these Chinese! The "foo can" is useful if you want to vanish water or rice. It may be used in combination with the Rice Bowls, or the funnel trick, described elsewhere. It has a secret compartment that retains a considerable amount of water when you invert the can (Fig. 91). The inner compartment "A" retains water or rice when the can is inverted.

FIGURE 91

111

The Coin Rattle Box

When it becomes necessary to vanish a coin or a ring, simply drop it into this innocent looking little box and slide on the cover. As you give it to a member of the audience who has volunteered to help, merely shake the box and the coin is heard to rattle. Although the coin has already been stolen, the box will obligingly rattle any time the wizard gives it a shake. For "The Coin in the Nest of Boxes" trick, or any similar trick, this inexpensive device is a good investment.

Magician's Wax

Wax is useful in many ways, especially for card tricks. It is sold by all dealers.

Touch-Up Paint

This is available in flesh-color or dull black. Its uses are obvious.

CHAPTER SEVEN

FAVORITE STAGE TRICKS

If you are a beginner, you will find some of this material advanced and difficult. On the other hand, if you are an old-timer, many of these stage tricks will certainly not be new to you. All this proves that you can't please everybody! It is true, however, that an old trick is like an old friend; it stands the rigors of time. The only test to apply to these effects is the question, "Is it a good trick, one that audiences will enjoy?"

General Suggestion on Apparatus

It takes a real artist to handle magic apparatus properly. The simplest piece of apparatus may require the most careful practice in handling. It isn't the trick that counts so much as how you present it.

Rehearse your talk, if there is any, while manipulating the apparatus. You will thus be able to time your every move with the appropriate comment. A few brief, amusing side remarks are better than tiring, continuous chatter. The talk should be presented as though it were spontaneous. This calls for planning and practice. A real magician can take a simple trick and endow it with a great deal of charm; a beginner will operate a costly illusion, yet the result may be awful.

Magic dealers carry a bewildering array of effects, all glowingly advertised. Actually the dealers give full value, when we consider that they are selling not only the apparatus, but also the secret of how the trick is done, and often their services, describing the routine and how best to present it.

It would be a good idea for the novice to get the advice of an experienced magician before spending money on apparatus. Magic dealers do not exchange goods, unless defective; and it would be unreasonable to expect it otherwise, for you get the secret with the trick. It is best, therefore, to exercise care and judgment in acquiring mechanical effects. Buy apparatus that is useful and practical and that goes with your ability and with your act.

Magic apparatus is best bought. Home-made gadgets generally look cheap and crude unless one is an expert craftsman. Ready made apparatus has a professional appearance, is durable and generally satisfactory.

Milk Pitcher and Confetti

This trick is quite amusing. In effect you pour a pitcher of milk into a paper cup. The milk vanishes and the cup is filled with confetti and paper ribbons.

The trick lies in a mechanical pitcher obtainable at low cost from all dealers. When you pour, you hold the spout of the pitcher against a large paper cup, the milk seems to vanish from the pitcher into the cup. The illusion is perfect.

The confetti is in the cup all the time. After pouring the milk, take a fan and fan the cup, tipping and shaking it slightly. The confetti floats into the air, making a beautiful picture. For a flash effect produce a small paper roll contained at the bottom of the cup. Silks may be "loaded" under cover of this paper ribbon, if desired. For a final finish throw the cup into the audience. I am indebted for this idea, in part, to an article by that clever wizard, Hen Fetsch, published in "The Sphinx."

The Restored Chinese Paper

Burning and restoring a strip of paper is a trick as old as the hills. The effect is wonderful. The following routine, known to professional magicians, is recommended. The paper, brightly colored, is about eighteen inches long and three inches wide. It is not prepared. There is a candle burning on a table at your right. A duplicate paper is pleated and tucked into a paper clip. This clip is attached under the left side of your coat with a safety pin. You may prefer the left coat lapel, or the flap of your left coat pocket.

Show the paper and show unmistakably empty hands. Hold one end of the paper in your right hand and ignite the paper in the candle flame. Retain it until nearly burned out, then release. It will float up, and drop downward. At this moment get the duplicate in your left hand. The misdirection is very good, for all eyes watch the flame as it devours the paper. Now, with a decisive motion, snatch into the floating ashes with your right hand, and pretend to deposit something in your open left palm which contains the duplicate. You are facing right.

The left hand is palm upward, the angle being such that the audience sees nothing. Peer into the palm and show surprise. Then swiftly draw upward the duplicate paper. This trick should be performed to music. It is a good opening number.

Be careful of low ceilings and possible fire risk.

The Borrowed Ring in the Dove Pan

The dove pan is described in the chapter on silk production. Here is another way to use this pan. A lady's ring is borrowed. This is hammered out of shape and caused to vanish into the barrel of a revolver. A metal pan or chafing dish is shown, a fire lighted in it. It is covered and a revolver fired at it. The pan is found to be full of flowers. These are presented to the lady; attached to these flowers by a silk ribbon is the borrowed ring.

Now for the working of the effect. As your assistant hands you the hammer with which to seemingly ruin the borrowed ring, you pass him this ring. A duplicate ring is hammered and apparently loaded into the gun, while your assistant is loading the flowers and the real ring into the cover of the dove pan. This he brings out and sets up ready for you to operate. The "load" is all in the cover. Alcohol in the pan serves as fuel. You can ignite a paper napkin if you prefer.

Clap the cover on, then fire the gun at the dove pan. Now take the cover off. Your trick is done. You may prefer to vanish the ring by use of the Rattle Box described in the "Accessories" chapter.

The Bottle and Glass — The "Passe Bottles"

This old and excellent trick still amuses audiences. Show a bottle and a glass, and pour liquid from one into the other. As these two objects are covered with two empty tubes, they strangely change places — then change back again.

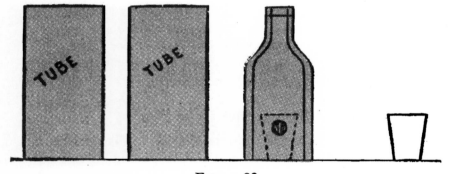

FIGURE 92

The bottle is not one, but two, one within the other, made and painted to look real. Each bottle has a hole in the back (Fig. 92). Through this hole you can control a concealed glass with your finger. The bottles are bottomless. At the start one bottle is within the other, one of the two glasses underneath. The other glass is on the table in plain sight. The tubes at this point may be passed for inspection for they are empty, and innocent. Remark, as you fit a tube over the outer bottle, "You see that the tube fits neatly over the bottle in this

116

manner." As you say this, draw off the outer bottle, using a forefinger, there being a hole also in the top of each covering tube for this purpose. Put the loaded tube over the visible glass to the left, and place the empty tube over the bottle to the right. Snap your fingers; utter a magic word or two; now pick up the right hand bottle, showing the glass underneath. Show the bottle on the left. To make them change back, merely reverse the process. Either bottle or glass may be shown at will, in either location.

The Production of a Goblet of Water

Expose both sides of a small foulard or scarf. This is now draped over your palm. Suddenly something rises in the hand, and upon removing the foulard a large goblet of water is visible.

The goblet is originally concealed under your coat, held in place with your left arm, or tucked under your suspenders. A rubber cover, obtainable from all magic dealers, will prevent the water from spilling when you hold the goblet bottom up. Show both sides of the foulard, and drape it over your left arm which is held in front of the body. At the same time get the goblet in your right hand, and drape the scarf over it, the hand palm up, and the goblet held bottom up, the slender stem between your fingers. With a sweeping motion suddenly reverse the goblet, slipping the cover off as you remove the scarf. This effect is very pretty.

Production of Goldfish Bowls

These are flat glass bowls, and may contain real goldfish. Rubber covers are furnished with them. The bowls are held in a shallow pocket under the arm and produced from beneath a scarf, as has been explained for the production of the goblet of water. With the "Abbott" bowl all the water is sealed in, as long as the bowl is vertical. No rubber cover is needed.

The Chinese Rice Bowls

This trick should be performed in Chinese costume, with oriental color and atmosphere. Two small bowls are shown to be empty by inverting them over a tray. One of the bowls (Fig. 93A) is then filled with rice and levelled off with a fan. The other bowl is inverted over the first one, and a few passes and incantations are made. As the upper bowl is removed, it is observed that there is now twice as much rice in the lower bowl. The bowls are once more put mouth to mouth, and after a few words in make-believe Chinese the bowls are seen to be filled with water, all the rice having vanished. The water is poured from bowl to bowl. The Chinese wonder-worker takes a deep bow.

One of the bowls is full of water at the start, but a celluloid circular disc keeps the water from pouring out when the bowl is turned over (Fig. 94). Scatter a few grains of rice on the tray to prevent the disk from sticking down. The water-bowl is put over the rice-bowl (Fig. 95), and in the course of saying Chinese prayers the two bowls are inverted, the rice bowl on top (Fig. 96). When the upper bowl is removed, a lot of rice pours out, as if the rice had doubled in bulk (Fig. 97). Level off the surplus rice with a fan. The disc is now slipped off (under cover of the fan) onto the tray with the rice, and the magician walks forward with the water, which he pours from bowl to bowl (Fig. 98). With the "Al Baker" method, no disk is required. It is very good.

Production of Paper Flowers

Make a cone of paper, and having demonstrated this to be empty, produce from it an incredible number of paper flowers of all colors. The secret is in the flowers. These are compressible, and contain a spring that pops them open to quite a large size. The flowers vary in cost, depending on size and quality. They are well worth acquiring, for they make a colorful and delightful illusion.

118

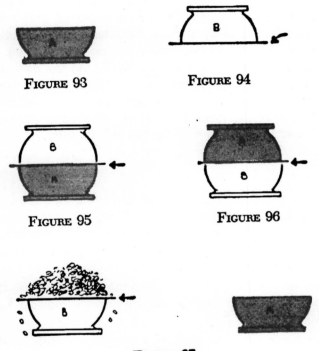

FIGURE 93

FIGURE 94

FIGURE 95

FIGURE 96

FIGURE 97

FIGURE 98

The flowers are held together by a small metal clip which opens when you squeeze the cone. A band of paper may hold them together which you break when taking the first flower out. There are various ways of getting possession of the packets of flowers. One good way is to have a packet under both upper sides of your vest, a black horsehair loop projecting from each. As you show both sides of your paper cone, get your thumb through one of the loops, and hold the packet by this loop behind the paper, dropping it into the cone, or wrapping the cone around it. Load the second packet under cover of the cone. It is also possible to have a U-shaped slit in the cone, and load the flowers directly through its side.

The Flag and the Candle

Produce a flag from the flame of a candle, and cause the flag to vanish between your hands. Wrap a piece of paper around the lighted candle. The wrapped candle is now broken, and there within is the vanished flag. Now create laughter by bringing a lighted candle from your pocket.

This delightful illusion will please any audience. It is carried out in a snappy tempo and requires a musical background.

The candle is a hollow shell of glossy paper with a bit of real candle at top and bottom. A duplicate flag is contained therein. At the start you have this candle burning on a table to your right. Wear a handkerchief "pull" on your right side. Your coat pocket contains a duplicate candle, and attached to the wick is a small match. A piece of sandpaper is glued onto the lining of your coat pocket near the top. A small rolled-up flag is palmed in your left hand. There is a piece of paper on the table.

After making a few passes over the candle, reach into the flame and produce the palmed silk from your left hand. At once, your right hand brings out the pull and works the silk into it. For a final move of the vanish pretend to throw the silk into the flame of the candle.

Now wrap the candle in the piece of paper. You can knock this candle on the table to prove that it is solid. It will give quite a convincing thump. When you tear the paper apart, the duplicate silk appears mysteriously. As you produce the candle from your pocket, strike it on the sandpaper just as you would a match, and under cover of your coat, bring it lighted into view. Place it in the empty candlestick. Dealers sell excellent fake candles and paper shells for this trick.

The Oriental Lota Jar

A metal water jar is shown to be empty. When turned over however, a quantity of water pours out. Several times during the act you suddenly spy more water in the jar. Pour this out quite forcefully, again and again, still the jar fills up with water.

The Lota jar has a number of small holes in the top. It is double, and contains several compartments, each controlled by one of the holes. A bit of wax (or adhesive tape) is placed over each hole. As long as the wax remains the water will not appear, but if you remove the wax the pressure of the air permits the water to run out. This device creates hilarious laughter, if properly worked. The performer always appears as much surprised as the audience.

The new "Grant" lota is perhaps the best of all. This vase may be passed around for inspection. Its capacity is surprising.

The Chinese Rings

There is no trick in magic which is more scientific than the Chinese Rings. The trick offers an infinite number of variations.

The set generally consists of eight metal rings. These may be passed out for inspection. However, you can always link them and unlink them with ease. Varied and attractive designs are available: the lotus, the butterfly, geometrical designs, chains, and the like. Purchase your rings from a dealer who will give you instructions at the same time.

If you desire to study this phase of magic in detail, there are several good books on the subject: Hoffman's, "Modern Magic," which every magician should own; Victor Farelli's, "The Odin Rings," a translation from the French; Namreh's, "Lincoln Rings;" also, "Clever Ring Routines" by the Ireland Magic Company of Chicago, and Professor Jack Miller's work. The Chinese Rings are not simply a trick. They are a complete act in themselves, fascinating and interesting. It would be impossible to cover even a small part of the subject here, for only a complete book can describe the operation of these rings. We are merely listing the subject, principally because of its importance in the world of magic. However, one thing we will emphasize — every magician ultimately works out his own ring combinations.

The Candle and the Bouquet

Color and beauty help make any illusion attractive to an audience. For this reason magic tricks with flowers are particularly worth while. One of these, the Candle and Bouquet is simple, yet beautiful. Toss a silk over a lighted candle. It changes at once into a beautiful bouquet of flowers which is much taller than the candle.

The trick is easy — the candle being merely a shell, contains within it a stand of brightly colored feathered flowers. These are compressed, and make an impressive showing when produced. This is done by pulling the outside shell off under cover of a foulard. For a finale produce a lighted candle from your pocket, as explained in "The Flag in the Candle." You thus complete the trick in an artistic manner.

The Floating Ball of Paper

Crush a larger sheet of tissue paper into a ball and mysteriously make it float in the air. You can pass a solid hoop around the ball while it floats. The effect is a beautiful illusion.

Make use of the magician's old stand-by — black thread, and have it as fine as possible. Pin one end of the thread to your table, and put a small waxed loop in the other end. As you place the solid hoop over your head, onto your shoulders, secretly hook the loop of waxed thread over one of your ears (the one farthest from the audience), and walk away from the table. Now you are ready to start. Crush the paper around the thread so that when your ball is finished, it is well wrapped around the thread, and will not slide. As you slowly let go of the ball it will seem to float in the air.

You approach the ball, it slowly falls. You back away and it rises. Wave one hand above the ball to seemingly command it to obey you. Use music for this effect.

The hoop can now be passed around the ball, then return it to your shoulders. Detach the thread from your ear, as you replace the hoop. Toss the paper onto your table, and go ahead with the next trick.

The Chinese Laundry Ticket

This is what magicians call a "fake expose," for you seem to explain a trick, but really don't. You come forward with a large tissue-paper laundry ticket in your left hand. (The writer's tickets are six inches by twenty, yellow paper stencilled with a row of Chinese letters.) The story and action are like this:

"It's fun to see a magic show, but it's still more fun to learn how a trick is done. This is going to be a lesson in magic. You have all seen a magician tear up a strip of paper, scatter a little woffle dust on it, then magically restore the paper. (As you refer to the woffle dust, put your hand in your right pants pocket and pretend to scatter some imaginary dust on the Chinese ticket. This leads up to a similar motion later.)

"Actually I'm not going to do the trick. I'm merely giving

the explanation. We use this large Chinese laundry ticket for the explanation. When the magician takes the ticket from the table, he also picks up another one at the same time. It is rolled in a ball, and you never see it because he turns his hand away, like this." (Actually show two tickets in your left hand rolled separately, but bunched together. Do not show them palmed, but merely held by one finger, thus you don't expose palming.)

"Now the magician tears the ticket into many pieces, like this. Then he rolls the pieces into a ball, but all the time you never see the extra ticket held in his hand." (Tear it, then roll it into a ball with the right palm, palming it off in the right hand. Also under cover of your right hand, separate the two rolls in your left hand so they are well apart, one in the finger tips, the other held in the left palm in plain sight. This you point to, which gives you a good excuse for the closed right hand. The audience assumes that the roll at the finger tips consists of the torn pieces).

"Now comes the dirty work. The magician *exchanges* the torn pieces for the whole ticket. Of course, he scatters a little woffle dust on it and the ticket is restored." (Slowly and openly exchange one roll for the other, using the left hand only. Then deliberately again reach into your right pants pocket for the woffle dust, leaving the torn pieces there, preferably in the upper "dead" section of the pocket. Be sure not to bring the right hand near the left when you scatter the woffle dust. Actually this trick is done almost wholly with the left hand. Now unroll the ticket, and toss it aside).

"It's a good trick. The band plays. The audience applauds. They send flowers up the aisles. But the hard part is how to get rid of the torn pieces." (Open up the supposedly torn pieces.) "You just blow on 'em . . . then open them up from north to south, . . . and from east to west, . . . and you don't have any trouble getting rid of the torn pieces. Thank you, folks."

Note, by this method we get away from the tedious method of first doing the trick, and then repeating it with the explanation. To the writer, this is repetitious and unnecessary. This interesting expose is also effective when done with paper napkins borrowed at any affair. Simply steal one in advance and hold it rolled in the left palm. Borrow two more, openly, and you are all set for a minor miracle.

The Sun and Moon Trick — For Laughs

Each magician performs this popular comedy trick in his own way. This one is audience-tested. The effect will be described as we go along. First make the following preparation:

In a "changing bag" on your left table, place a red bandanna handkerchief, placing also a cheap, white one in the opposite compartment. The red one should be in the open section. On the same table, lay a folded, duplicate, red bandanna, its center cut out in a round hole three inches in diameter. This center is attached to the folded handkerchief with a rubber band, as in the sketch. Place a pair of scissors on the same table.

On the right table, place a box servante, containing two handkerchiefs, a red and a white, rolled together, the red one

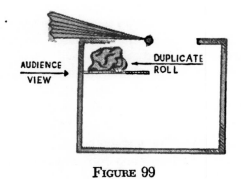

AUDIENCE VIEW → | DUPLICATE ← ROLL

FIGURE 99

125

on the outside. One is a red duplicate bandanna with a white center sewed in. The other is a white duplicate with a red center sewed in. They are secured by a rubber band. A "break-away" fan lies on the box servante (Fig. 99).

Call two boys forward. One must have a clean, white handkerchief. This you promptly put into the "changing bag" alongside the red one, switching the bag. Take the duplicate white one out, saying, "Perhaps you would rather see your handkerchief all the time?" Hand it to the boy on the right, crumpling it to prevent recognition. Take the scissors and explain to him that if he says the right magic word he can cut any article and restore it. Pull up the center of the handkerchief and illustrate by actually cutting out this center. Have him say a magic word to restore it. Nothing happens. Blame it on the boy. Put your hand through the hole and look worried. Observe, "Well, anyhow, it's nice to have met you." Tell him not to get his nose through the hole.

Bring forward your red handkerchief with the center cut, but attached. It appears whole. Say, "Well, since I have spoiled yours, I shall do the same to my own. They say that misery loves company." Pretend to cut out the red center and show it cut out. The rubber band is now on your fingers. Give the two cut centers to the boy on the right. Now roll up the two mutilated handkerchiefs, the red one on the outside, to resemble the roll in the box servante. Secure this with the rubber band. Remark, "We shall restore these with the magic fan. Have you seen my magic fan? It was given to me by an old Chinese magician, named Ah Phooey." Hold the rolled-up handkerchiefs between the first and second fingers of your right hand. As you pick up the fan with both hands, drop this roll inside the box servante and get the duplicate roll with the thumb and first finger of your right hand, under cover of the fan. This switch takes a second.

Bring the fan and the bandanna roll forward, calling attention to the magic fan, and casually giving the roll to the boy on the left. Take the two cut out centers (in your left hand) from the boy and give him the fan in exchange. Tell him to wave the magic fan above the centers. Explain that they will vanish and reappear in their rightful places, with the cut handkerchiefs completely restored. The "breakaway" fan falls apart when opened by the boy, but it works all right when you open it. For a time stir up some fun with the boy and the fan. Finally, conclude that the boy is "no magician," and vanish the centers, with a pull or a pocket vanish. Now have the handkerchiefs opened, meanwhile assuring your audience cheerfully that all is well; but how chagrined and upset you become to find that there is a red center in the white handkerchief and vice versa. Pace up and down, and tell the boy on the right that it is all his fault. Meanwhile, hold these handkerchiefs up high and wide, so that everybody will appreciate the joke. It does get a hearty laugh.

Now get the "changing bag." Tell the boy on the left that he is probably a better magician. Place the mismatched handkerchiefs in the empty half of the bag and switch it. Tell the boy to pass his hand over the bag, saying, "Merry Christmas." You retort, "Happy New Year." Now take out the borrowed, white handkerchief, returning it to its owner. Produce the red bandanna, and make a good showing of it. Take your bow.

Lightning Source UK Ltd.
Milton Keynes UK

178110UK00001B/153/P